The Legacy of a Sow's Ear

The saying goes that "you cannot
make a silk purse from a sow's ear".
The geniuses at Arthur D. Little, Inc.
disproved it. However, they did not
know that the purse they produced
would not last.
Neither did the Company.

Ivars Avots

The Legacy of
a Sow's Ear

The Rise and Fall of Arthur D. Little, Inc.

Trans-Global Management
2004

Published in the United States by Trans-Global Management Systems, Inc.

Copyright © 2004 by Trans-Global Management Systems, Inc.

Library of Congress Cataloging-in-Publication Data are available

ISBN 0–9754603–0–7

9 8 7 6 5 4 3 2 1

Preface

The author was at Arthur D. Little, Inc. (ADL) from 1964 to 1981 and had a good feel for the pulse of the Company during that time. To describe the following two decades that led to the demise of the Company, he had to turn to colleagues who had stayed on. While many of them provided useful information, it needed a lot of interpretation.

First, many of the former ADLers were getting old and their recollections of the events they had experienced often were dim.

Second, many ADLers still felt strongly about personal alliances they had formed over the years and were defensive about saying anything that would reflect badly on their friends.

Third, some former key executives declined to comment at all. Some were under court orders not to talk; others feared that they may still find themselves the subject of a lawsuit.

Fourth, the ADLers who suffered a financial loss because of the bankruptcy, were bitter about the ADL leadership and their recollections may have been tainted.

Finally, as former CEO John Magee remarked about the people contemplating a book about the Company, "Everybody has his own opinion." The author of this book clearly has his own opinion, as well, and although he has tried to keep it out of the manuscript, he may not have succeeded completely.

As a result, the book reflects the opinions, biases, and different views one may find in any organization as diverse as ADL. At the same time, it provides an unadulterated glimpse into a consulting firm that left its mark in the history of American business.

Acknowlegments

Many former ADLers contributed to this book through interviews, e-mails and written materials. Some reviewed specific chapters and others helped to select an appropriate title.

Valuable contributions were made by Richard Caro, John Carter, Dianne Cermak, Martha Cotton, Todd DeBinder, Jean deValpine, Tamara Erickson, Tray Evarts, Harry Foden, Stephen Grey, Alma Triner Hagel, Richard Heitman, Theodore Heuchling, Harry Lambe, Julie Lang, Melvyn Klein, Suford Lewis, Craig Lentz, Stephen Low, Demos Menegakis, Richard Messing, Peter Metz, Michael Michaelis, Jan Niemans, William O'Neil, Irving Plotkin, Harland Riker, Terry Rothermel, Paul Schoenemann, Roger Shamel, Ed Shanley, Arthur Solomon, Nicholas Steinthal, John Stevenson, Jeff Traenkle, Frank Yans, Lou Visco, Joe Voci, Cheryl Walsh and Al Wechsler.

Jean Harrison, Ingrid Silberman, and Juliette Avots helped with the editing, Standish Bradford Jr. advised on legal issues, and Larry Prusak gave much needed encouragement as the first reader of the manuscript. Noted Latvian cartoonist Romans Vitkovskis came up with imaginative illustrations. Ligita Liepa applied her publishing expertise to convert the manuscript into a book.

Contents

Introduction

For more than a century, the name of Arthur D. Little commanded respect from executives and government officials around the globe. They called on the consulting firm bearing the name of its founder for help in solving knotty technological problems, as well as planning the economies of entire nations. Then, within a single decade, the prestigious company turned into an "also-ran" that could not extract itself from a financial quagmire and was sold off piecemeal by the bankruptcy court.

Companies do not get into trouble by themselves. As at Enron and MCI, it is usually a small group of people who make it happen. The company may continue to look good to the outsiders, and even its auditors may not see that the foundations are crumbling. Since Arthur D. Little, Inc. (ADL) was not a publicly traded company, there was no outside interest to see what was going on. There was no Warren Buffett to jump on the board of directors when the company made poor management and financial decisions.

The handful of people who were responsible for guiding ADL were a product of ADL's own environment, which had been evolving over decades. The emphasis changed from technology to management, but chemists and mathematicians were at the helm. This was similar to The Boeing Company where, prior to the very successful 747 project, nearly all the executives were aeronautical engineers. Boeing started to change and diversify only after Frank Schrontz, a lawyer, became the CEO.[1] The ADL executives espoused change, but while its competitors grew and prospered in the seventies and eighties, they never took the steps that would lead to significant changes.

---

[1] Ironically, Boeing started running into serious management problems as soon as another aeronautical engineer, Phil Condit, replaced Schrontz. By 2003, when Condit resigned, Boeing had lost much of its one-time glamour.

This book is not an analysis of what went wrong at ADL. It sets a perspective on the company, as it evolved and as it went down. It then goes behind the formal facade and shows ADL as it is remembered by its former managers and staff members. The book does not assign blame for the Company's demise to any of its leaders. It does, however, illustrate their personalities through reported actions and anecdotes. The reader can make his or her own conclusions.

In "Final Accounting," the story of Arthur Andersen's fall from grace, Barbara Ley Toffler states that the demise of the once prestigious firm began long before its involvement with Enron. It was an inflexible corporate culture where independent activities were not tolerated or encouraged. When its leaders lost a sense of decency and integrity, the culture that had valued conformity ended in disaster.

The fall of Arthur D. Little was also set in motion long before the bankruptcy, and some of the reasons were similar. Although ADL housed many independent talents, its conservative culture discouraged activities that could have helped it keep up with the changing consulting business. While its leaders cannot be accused of lacking integrity, they stayed on a narrow track that was leading the Company nowhere. Like the senior partners at Arthur Andersen, a few of them made a lot of money for themselves. The most loyal employees, who stayed until the end, came out losers.

CHAPTER 1

Starting Up

On October 1, 1886, Arthur Dehon Little, a young chemist who had dropped out of the Massachusetts Institute of Technology, opened a laboratory in downtown Boston. In a letter home to his father, he noted that he and his partner, Roger Griffin, would probably have little to do in the first six months, but from then on the business should do well. The laboratory offered chemical examinations and analyses of a wide variety of compounds. Such services had become important for a growing number of merchants and manufacturers who were increasingly purchasing supplies from a distance and were concerned about their purity.

Arthur D. Little had studied chemistry at MIT but had not graduated because he could not afford the tuition. He had taken a job as a chemist and file clerk at the Richmond Paper Company in Rumford, Rhode Island. Soon he was running the mill for the absent owners, and inventing digesters and other equipment for the paper industry. It was also here where he met Roger Griffin, his future business partner.

Success for the new company, know as Griffin and Little, did not come as soon as expected and it was a long time before Little was able to make a good living. Seven years after the Company was founded, Roger Griffin died tragically in a laboratory explosion. Little continued as a consultant and became involved in two new synthetics—cellulose nitrate and cellulose acetate—which were being used for photographic film and woven fabrics. Despite his international reputation as a problem solver and consultant in a number of fields, Arthur D. Little operated on a shoestring for the first 25 years.

As Europeans started up plants in the U.S. using the new technologies, Little became interested in their business approach. He could not understand why American financiers were reluctant to undertake technology ventures and mounted a writing and speaking campaign directed at financial, political, and educational leaders to encourage the nascent American chemical industry. Companies began to hire him for advice on how best to construct factories and manage production.

Little was also an environmentalist and believed that American businesses were squandering valuable resources. He was one of the first to warn of a society that would destroy its own environment. He once calculated that each year Americans wasted 150 million tons of wood, 1 million tons of flax straw, 365 billion cubic feet of natural gas, and 13 million board feet of lumber just from discarding old pencil stubs. He began advising businesses on how they could do more with byproducts, such as sugarcane bagasse that could be turned into paper.

Little's thrust took another turn in 1900 when he formed a new partnership with William H. Walker, a young MIT chemistry instructor. When Walker was recalled to MIT to reform the chemical engineering curriculum, Little supported him by gaining approval and funds for various initiatives to bring industry and education closer together. In 1908, these efforts led to the formation of MIT's Research Laboratory of Applied Chemistry. It was supported by various chemical companies that supplied fellowships to chemical engineering students who worked on real industrial problems.

For the next few years, Arthur D. Little and William Walker remained deeply involved with MIT in defining chemical engineering as a separate profession with a distinct approach and training method. During that period, the ideal chemical engineer could move from industry to industry, mixing and matching the various operations that Little was later to call "unit operations." The new approach changed the emphasis from traditional industrial chemistry and mechanical engineering to the unit-operations laboratory. Along the way, Arthur D. Little made up for dropping out of school when MIT awarded him with an honorary doctor's degree.

Since he started his first laboratory with Roger Griffin, the griffin had been used as the company logo. In 1916, Dr. Little changed it to an acorn with wings. It is said that he had adopted a winged maple leaf for a Canadian subsidiary and wanted the parent Company to have something similar. The flying acorn remained ADL's symbol for about six decades despite the fact that, with the advent of airplane travel, its consultants were sometimes called "flying nuts."[1]

As a result of Little's keen sense for promotion, the Company that he had started prospered and gained in reputation. It received national recognition in 1921 when Dr. Little set out to disprove the popular saying that you cannot make a silk purse out of a sow's ear. A hundred pounds of sows' ears were procured from a Chicago meat-

---

[1] The acorn symbol was finally brought down by complaints from the Paris office that pointed out its French significance as a low-class sex symbol.

packer. Two ADL chemists pared them down to ten pounds of a glue-like viscous material. They then forced the material through fine holes to produce a thread, but found that the product was far too brittle for knitting. After some experimentation, they found that a glycerin solution would soften the threads and permit them to be woven into a silky material. They produced two colorful purses that became symbols of technological achievement. One of them was presented to the Smithsonian Institution in 1977.

Along with success came a certain amount of arrogance that characterized ADL throughout its lifetime. There was an underlying feeling that ADL was the best and, with the exception of MIT, it did not need to cooperate with others. When the Association of Management Consulting Firms (formerly ACME) was founded in 1929 and the Company was invited to join, Dr. Little declared that ADL was neither a firm of management consultants nor management engineers and would not benefit from joining an industry association.

When Dr. Little died in 1935, he left his controlling shares in ADL to a trust for the benefit of his *alma mater*, MIT. His nephew Royal Little, a leading American industrialist in his own right, became the sole trustee and Chairman of the Board of Directors of ADL. Although ADL claimed to be the first and the oldest management consulting firm in the United States, others viewed this event as the true beginning of ADL as a major consulting organization. That viewpoint would support the claim of McKinsey, having started in 1926, as the nation's oldest management consulting firm.

Carrying on the technology tradition

The man following Dr. Little's footsteps was Earl Stevenson who had joined ADL after World War I where he had served as a lieutenant in the U.S. Army Chemical Corps. He was a practicing chemist with a master's degree from MIT. He resonated well with Dr. Little and became research director a year later. He is said to have been very prudent, so that when he became president in 1935, he insisted that staff members answer their own telephones and travel at night so as not to waste useful daylight hours.

A year after Stevenson's arrival, he was joined by another MIT chemist, Raymond Stevens. While Stevenson was primarily a scientist, Stevens was primarily a salesman. The two new executives were very useful to Dr. Little who had come under criticism for his carefree handling of financial affairs while the Company was having a hard time. Stevens followed Stevenson up the career ladder and succeeded him as president.

The emphasis on technology continued until the fifties when ADL employed about 125 people, all of them with technical degrees. The first staff member to break this practice was John "Zip" Stevenson who was a history major with a Harvard MBA degree. After having been hired by ADL, he was surprised to find that the Company had a close relationship with MIT and that its professors participated in many of ADL's cases.[2]

Technology under fire

By 1969, ADL had gained the reputation as one of the leading management consulting firms in America. It had a staff of about 1600 employees, more than half of whom were professionally trained scientists, engineers, economists, and management specialists. In addition, ADL had contract relationships with more than 350 consultants, drawn primarily from universities, to provide specific skilled advice. The Company was in a unique position to build on these assets because it understood both technology and management practice—a combination that its competitors did not have, but clients wanted. Unfortunately, the technical side of the Company was apprehensive about the growth of the management area. Lacking

---

[2] "Zip" took advantage of this when he was placed in charge of a large economic development project for Puerto Rico. He engaged an MIT professor to teach business research to case team members whose technical background had not prepared them for analysis of business issues. This resulted in greater consistency and better quality of work. In later years, newly hired staff members were expected to come already equipped with all the necessary knowledge.

7

support from all parts of the Company, management did not take advantage of its favorable competitive position.

At the same time that the evolving corporate system placed emphasis on immediate profits, it did not encourage technical people to introduce the next generation of technology or to train their successors. There were no incentives or awards for anything other than maximizing client billings. As an unfortunate result, when the technical people retired in subsequent years, the successful technology practices they had gradually built up often disappeared with them.

Although ADL developed many technologies that were highly valued in the market, it did not learn to make money from them other than through client billings. Typically, ventures that were developed within ADL did not come to fruition until they were separated from the Company. For example, Cryogenics Technology did not thrive until it was split from ADL. ADL Pipe was an engineering software activity that performed much better after it was spun off. A possible explanation for this situation was the culture clash between those who valued creativity and problem solving and those who pursued hard business.[3]

The sunset for technology

ADL's work in research and development management covered a span of 120 years. Starting in 1880, ADL began promoting the importance of R&D to achieve corporate economic growth. A hundred years later, many U.S. corporations and government agencies began to initiate R&D activities, and ADL was well- qualified to assist. It introduced a technical audit service which was aimed at assisting industries and government agencies in adopting best practices in the organization and administration of R&D. This service eventually became a continuing business. Studies aimed at improving R&D organization and administration were carried out for more than 200 industrial clients and several government agencies.

---

[3] In the mid-eighties, ADL launched Critical Fluid Systems, a subsidiary based on a new technology that would enable the Company to become a major player in the field of hazardous waste processing. However, the startup incurred substantial losses and was abandoned a few years later.

The R&D activity, or TPD (Technology & Product Development) as it was later called, continued to be the strongest asset of ADL, even as management tried to move away from the application of technology and become more like McKinsey. To give a boost to its technology reputation, some ADLers wanted to have a publicity event similar to the feat of making a silk purse out of a sow's ear some 50 years earlier. One idea was to disprove the assumption that lead balloons cannot fly. Eventually, three teams of ADL staff built lead balloons and competed as to whose would fly furthest. One of the balloons flew up so high that it caused alarms to go off on the radar screens at Boston's Logan airport.

The engineers figured that the surface area of a balloon increased as the square of its spherical diameter, while buoyancy and lift capacity increased as the cube of its spherical diameter. This meant that a lead balloon of any skin thickness could become buoyant when large enough and filled with helium.

The practical question was where to find the thinnest commercially available lead foil. It happened that a colleague had recently ordered such a foil for another project and the remainder still sat in his basement. With a supply of the foil in hand, the engineers undertook the task of calculating the most advantageous way of converting the flat material into shapes that could form a buoyant sphere.

One group acquired a weather balloon about ten feet in diameter to serve as a pattern, cut the lead foil into a seemingly interminable number of shapes and sizes, then glued these together to form a reasonably gas-tight, buoyant sphere. Another group chose to construct a large folding box of lead foil that self-unfolded when filled with helium. A third group constructed an elegant miniature dirigible of balsa wood, and then covered it with the lead foil.

Launch day was breezy. The first balloon rose successfully but brushed against a building during takeoff. The resulting small tear led to a loss of helium and a descent after a flight of about two miles. The inflatable box tore during filling and failed to rise. The dirigible took off successfully and eventually disappeared from sight.

In 1984, ADL itself was carried away by the arrival of artificial intelligence technology. Visualizing a market that would top $100 billion, the Company set up a group of about a dozen people to focus on the subject. Even Memorial Drive Trust, ADL's profit sharing and retirement plan, committed funds to these efforts. However, the artificial intelligence boom was short-lived and it never paid off for the Company.

In 1985, E.J. Kahn, Jr., the author of some two dozen books and a staff writer for the *New Yorker*, wrote a book, *The Problem Solvers*. It was the inside story of Arthur D. Little Inc., the Company that "helped industrialize Puerto Rico and developed antiknock gasoline, a Bloody Mary mix, buffered aspirin, a talking clock, charcoal briquettes, and instant breakfast." It was supposed to reflect the history of some 75,000 projects undertaken in 86 countries by what was then considered the world's leading management and technology consulting firm. Success stories followed one after another, and bigger things followed any occasional stumbles. But—the emphasis was definitely on research, even in management consulting activities.

By the early '90s, the management consulting advocates had gained the upper hand and TPD was beginning to be seen as a stepchild. The managers of the technology practice were not able to pull the teams together. The different units were acting independently and did not have a clear model for selling their services. It was ironic that, ten years later, this stepchild would become the only part of ADL to survive.

CHAPTER 2

Memorial Drive Trust

Twice a year, former employees of ADL piled into the cafeteria at Acorn Park to hear a presentation on the status of the MDT – Memorial Drive Trust. There were hundreds of them, mostly grey-haired, often pot-bellied, but always with a sparkle in the eyes. They included not only former staff members, but also secretaries and maintenance workers who had spent most of their lives taking care of ADL. Now, MDT was taking care of them. As one observer noted, "I have never seen so many millionaires together in one room."

In 1951, Royal Little noticed that two organizations, Battelle Memorial Institute and Stanford Research Institute, were increasingly outbidding ADL on research assignments. Since both of these were not-for-profit institutes, Royal Little looked for a way to make ADL more competitive by reducing its own taxes. In addition, he was concerned about the break-up of the majority holding after his death. He strongly desired to find a mechanism by which unifying control of the company could be kept intact, in good hands, so that the ethical concepts, business policies, and particularly ADL's truly unique blend of pioneering, free enterprise spirit with high intellectual and professional standards might long survive him.

Taking advantage of newly issued laws, he set up the Memorial Drive Trust (MDT) combining the tax saving, succession, and employee incentive features. Half of the Company's pretax earnings were allocated to the trust for the benefit of ADL employees. This was as large a share of profits as stockholders had ever allocated to employees in any American company, and was a far larger proportion than the norm among profit-sharing companies.

In addition to serving as a tax-saving tool and a profit-sharing trust for ADL employees, MDT came in handy for reducing the outside control over the Company.[1] With loans from the Bank of Boston, MDT purchased the controlling shares of ADL that had been held by the MIT trust, and over the next few years swept up all remaining minority shares. By 1960, MDT held all the ADL stock.

To manage MDT as well as other trusts associated with Textron[2] and affiliated companies, Royal Little hired Jean deValpine. Little had played tennis with the young man at the Boston Tennis and Racquet Club and respected his master's degree in engineering, as well as his degree from Harvard Law School. DeValpine soon was appointed chief executive officer of MDT which was then worth about $10 million and consisted mainly of ADL stock and the Acorn Park facilities.

To set a public benchmark for valuing the ADL shares held by MDT, Royal Little wanted to establish a public market for them. In 1969, thirty percent of ADL shares were sold to the public through an underwritten offering. As a part of this process, ADL discovered that the lawyer who drew up the incorporation papers sixty years earlier had accounted for only half of the $10,000 in capital assets it was supposed to have.[3] Although this meant that technically ADL had never legally existed, it did not interfere with the offering.

The ADL-MDT institutional structure worked effectively until 1987 when a group formed by Plenum-Bear Stearns-Skadden Arps made an attempt to take over ADL. Nobody understood why Plenum, a publishing company, would be interested in a consulting firm, except that they may have viewed the ADL stock as undervalued. After Plenum offered about ten percent over the market value of the stock, the MDT trustees were faced with the fiduciary responsibility of sell-

---

[1] The MIT trust owned 55% of ADL.
[2] In 1923, Royal Little borrowed $10,000 to launch the Special Yarns Corporation that eventually evolved into Textron—sometimes considered to be the first industrial conglomerate.
[3] The error can be traced back to a young lawyer, Louis Brandeis, who later became a noted associate justice of the Supreme Court.

ing the stock if it was beneficial to the trust. Once they had gotten over the initial shock, the trustees declared that the current market price was just one indicator of the value of the Company. Consideration should also be given to its future potential and any effect a sale would have on the employees. Plenum responded with a somewhat higher bid but this was also rejected.

An experience that both ADL and MDT tried hard to forget was their involvement with Gerald Bull, the inventor of the superguns that eventually turned up in Saddam Hussein's inventory.

In the sixties, Bull was at McGill University in Montreal where he was a recognized expert in measuring the performance of objects in flight. Bernard Vonnegut, an ADLer and the brother of novelist Kurt Vonnegut, introduced him to ADL. This resulted in cooperative work on a NASA contract.

At McGill, Bull was expected to study the effect that meteorites had on space satellites. In fact, he was working on a military system to destroy incoming ballistic missiles, later seen in the Star Wars program. While studying at McGill, Bull found the German World War I plans for a gun that would terrorize the residents of Paris. The problem was that this gun would deliver a payload of only 15 pounds and need frequent maintenance.

After an accidental explosion in the basement of the McGill laboratory, Bull was forced to take his experiments elsewhere. He set up shop in a desolate area of Vermont on the Canadian border. At this remote site, Bull welded together two surplus naval canons and developed a suitable rocket propellant. It is not clear to what extent ADL helped him on this, but tests in Vermont and the Caribbean showed that the gun could deliver some 1300 pounds accurately over hundreds of miles.

The Vermont location also came in handy when Bull started work on a U.S./Canadian venture to develop huge guns capable of firing satellites into orbit. Land on the Canadian side was added to the property, resulting in a unique cross-border activity that exploited any legal differences that may have existed between Canada and the United States.

The "Long Tom," as it was called, was originally intended to put small payloads into orbit at a cost of only about $120,000 per launch. Unfortunately, by the time the experiments were completed, the U.S./Soviet space race had progressed to the point where Bull's invention was no longer needed. Not to be discouraged, Bull looked for military applications for his invention and found an interested client—Sadam Hussein.

Although the gun project was cancelled due to funding limitations, Bull emerged as one of the world's leading experts on ballistics. At the same time, ADL recognized the potential of his research and considered making an investment in the activity. Another potential investor was the Bronfman family of Seagram's fame.

General Gavin felt that Bull's research might present an opportunity for ADL. Consequently, Space Research Corporation (SRC) was formed, with ADL holding 51 percent of the shares. ADL was to provide the management skills while the Bronfman empire would provide the funds. Bronfman put up the first million outright, but required that any subsequent investments be shared equally by ADL. With the funding in hand, SRC showed much activity, but never achieved profitability.

When Royal Little decided to sell some ADL stock to the public, SRC and another ADL subsidiary—Cryogenic Technology Inc., were seen as undesirables on the balance sheet. SRC was turned over to MDT in the form of a dividend at a value of one dollar. Jean deValpine inadvertently ended up as the chairman of a small, unprofitable company in an otherwise exceptional investment portfolio.

Continuing to seek profitable assignments, Bull ventured into the arms trade with South Africa, but this did not prevent SRC debt to escalate to more than $9 million. Concerned with the continuing losses and shady business dealings that could reflect badly on MDT's reputation, deValpine resigned from the SRC board. A year later, MDT sold its stock in SRC for just ten dollars, and ADL noted that it had been a venture that, in retrospect, it would just as soon have never heard of.

ADL had severed its relationship with Bull just in time. In 1988 Iraq took delivery of a 350mm "Baby Baylon" that was capable of launching rocket-assisted shells with chemical, biological or nuclear warheads. Bull was also constructing two huge 1000mm guns. These guns were estimated to have a range of 200 miles, which caused considerable concern because they would have been able to hit targets in Israel.

Gerald Bull was assasinated in March 1990 by an apparently professional assailant, rumored to be an agent of the Israeli secret service. Soon after Bull's death, parts for a supergun that could fire shells over a distance of 2500 miles were seized in several European countries. They had been readied for illegal shipment to Iraq. Two completed guns were later found and destroyed by U.S. forces during the Gulf war.

It is believed that the Plenum attack failed because the group had not done its homework. They had expected to find at least some conflicting interests between ADL and MDT that would work in their favor. Extensive pleadings, depositions and discovery processes failed to produce such results. Jean deValpine believes that if Plenum had known that the structure would prove to be invulnerable, they would have approached MDT directly or might have sought an easier target elsewhere.

While the Plenum group did not succeed, it showed ADL how vulnerable it was to a takeover. As a result, the MDT plan needed to be amended. It was decided that MDT would hold no less than 51 percent of outstanding ADL shares. In disposing of any ADL shares, MDT would also consider any possible harmful effects on the professional environment afforded to the employee-beneficiaries of the trust.

To further avoid the possibility of takeover attempts ADL investigated various alternate ownership forms. Several issues had changed since the Company went public. One reason for going public had been to establish a market value for the ADL stock. This had been accomplished and was no longer an issue. The other reason had been to use the stock as a currency in acquisitions of other companies. This had not taken place to any significant extent and was not expected in the future. At the end, it was decided that the corporate structure would be maintained but the outstanding stock would be bought back and the Company would again become private.

Interestingly, the process did not go entirely without a hitch. Two lawsuits were filed: one that claimed that ADL did not pay enough for the stock and another that claimed it paid too much. Only one of the lawsuits made it to trial, and the Company prevailed.

Not every member of the MDT ended up as a millionaire. The trust actually included several funds, some with and some without ADL stock. The retirees could choose between funds that included up to 15% of ADL stock, but the current employees were restricted to a fund that consisted primarily of ADL stock. Employees who saw the writing on the wall left ADL and cashed in their MDT holdings. Those who stayed with ADL until the bitter end lost most of their savings when the stock became worthless.

CHAPTER 3

Life at Acorn Park

"Since coming to work for ADL, I have made friends in cities from coast to coast and abroad," a staff member noted. "I can point you to the best hotel rooms in Minneapolis, the best churrascaria in Rio, the best place to change money in Delhi. But I would be completely lost in Boston. If they do any business here, I have not heard of it."

In many ways, ADL was an introverted culture that had been self-perpetuating for over a century. People who did not fit into this culture moved on,[1] but others often stayed on until retirement. Initially shaped by chemical engineers, the culture favored scientists and mathematicians as top managers. ADL staff focused on the work at hand and did not get close to their clients.[2] To the outsiders they appeared formal and aloof. Some said ADLers had a macho attitude as if they were better than others and that it paralleled a similar attitude at MIT.

The Company's main facility at Acorn Park in Cambridge, Massachusetts, was isolated by a highway on one side and a brook on the other. Unlike the employees of downtown Boston companies, ADLers did not get outside their office environment. Nearby restaurant

---

[1] When one sales-oriented individual joined the Information Systems section, he brought in new cases and expected other staff members to work on them. Instead, he was accused of not paying attention to the staffers talents and interests. He resigned under pressure and later became the director of consulting operations for one of the big accounting firms.

[2] One senior staff member once visited a client together with an executive from McKinsey & Company. He was shocked to find that the competitor addressed the client executive by his first name and even kissed his wife.

facilities were limited, so that even at lunch ADLers would usually see only their colleagues. In some ways, it was like living in a small village in the middle of a desert.

Outsiders sometimes complained that ADL gave the appearance of being cold and somewhat above others. Inside, however, the ADL culture was reputed to have a "small town feel." "Even though the firm has thousands of employees in offices worldwide," one employee observed, "its collegial and entrepreneurial bent gives it a small company feel." ADL was also characterized as "a thousand companies of three," reflecting the average team size and the independent nature of the consulting work. One section head in the sixties used to characterize ADL as an office building shared by six hundred individual consultants.

During its growth years from the fifties through the seventies, ADL attracted many talented people who pursued their interests, sometimes without much relationship to their academic background. ADL was a flat organization where staff members were expected to direct their own career paths. Employees were smart and highly respected. Peer recognition motivated them more than anything else. "I think it's a great place to work," noted one consultant. "It has a key uniqueness—its technology heritage. It's fun to work on a case team with industry experts, functional experts, and technical experts." When ADL hired a new public relations director, she was very excited to learn about new things—about everything— she said the diversity was the engine of the Company.

Unlike almost every other organization, ADL exercised very little direct control and supervision of its staff. Because the most important motivator for the consultants was peer recognition if one wanted help in the form of direction from a superior, he had to ask for it. There seemed to be an unwritten tradition that each member of the staff was a competent professional who was thereby automatically capable of directing himself. This mode of organizational behavior was sometimes described as "benevolent anarchy."

The key to succeeding as a new employee was, in fact, making yourself known to case leaders. Since this was a well-worn path, most case leaders would usually invite a new employee for a chat. Occasionally this led to a few days work on a project. Newcomers tried to do the best they possibly could on the task and then, next time, get an even bigger piece of work, then a subcase, and so on. Pretty soon, a positive reputation would spread around and demands for the new employee's time would exceed his availability, opening the way for a pay and billing rate increase.

This simple system had a couple of great results:

- Individuals constantly got feedback on their work. Poor performers were washed out quickly as the system boosted star new hires long before formal performance reviews. This was like an internal market for the time and energy of smart people. To make sure enough information was floating around to let the market work, it needed things like the lead reports and people like Karl Klaussen, the Contracting Officer.

- The system provided safe and effective sales training for young people. However, it was also invisible to real clients, hence safe. It was effective, in the sense that one really did have to get on projects and stay billable or leave. It gave young people a chance to find out that selling could actually be fun, and it made case leaders king with a simple working formula: find your clients, scope and price the work, recruit a great case team, and run with it!

- For many years, there was no career ladder within the organization and titles meant little as new jobs allowed for a new hierarchical structure. Once a staff member developed a positive reputation, he could get to work on lots of different kinds of projects in different fields and explore the whole breath and depth of ADL's wide-ranging activities. In this sense, ADL was a remarkable place that knew how to embrace smart people and let them find their own growth paths in new directions.

An ADLer who joined the Company in the sixties remembers that his new boss told him that for the first six months he need not worry about billability since that was taken care through the government contract to which he was assigned. Instead, he was advised to get to know as many other staff members as possible. He was given a list of people to be invited to lunch so they could learn about his qualifications and invite him to join the cases they were undertaking. Consequently, when he was not inviting others to lunch, he found he was having lunch with others.

ADL's basic operational unit was the section, which functioned like a homeroom that could have as little or as much to do with one's day-to-day work as one liked. The only "rule" was to stay billable, which was not a problem as long as the economy demanded consultant services. A comment from a section head summed up this arrangement when he said: "We kick people off the dock. If they can swim, it is all right. If not, they belong somewhere else."

If a junior staff member was selected to be a case leader, he would usually form his team from his immediate section. More seasoned staff members looked all around the Company for the people most suited for the task. ADL was unique in that a junior staff member could have his boss working for him on a case, and could drop him any time, usually on the pretense that his budget required him to do so.

While the ADL culture encouraged innovation, it had to fit into a narrowly defined framework. People with truly entrepreneurial spirit were viewed with concern, were not encouraged to develop their ideas, and were not recommended for positions of higher responsibility. More than one staff member was held back from moving up in the Company by being described by his senior peers as "having too many ideas," "not projecting a conservative image," or "potentially committing the Company to half-baked projects."

Filtered through the lens of conservative professionals, ADLers did not make good managers in industry. This may be the reason why so few of them, in comparison to other consulting firms, moved to top-level positions in client companies. One of the more prominent ex-ADL consultants was Ray Gilmartin who joined Merck in 1994 and became its highly visible CEO. *The Wall Street Journal* noted about ten years later that Gilmartin had shown a sorry lack of vision in committing one of the greatest marketing blunders of the last decade. After inventing the first anticholesterol drug, Merck gave the market away to others and scorned big mergers that could have given it breathing room to weather patent expirations. The *Journal* concluded that, despite good current earnings, the long-range outlook for the company was grim.

When I joined ADL, I was assigned exclusively to a large Navy contract. When it expired a few years later, the involved staff members were reassigned to other departments in the Company. My field had been project management, and nobody outside the government area understood what it was. Since project management techniques involved computations, I was placed in the Operations Research group. Surrounded by top-class mathematicians and statisticians, I felt very much out of place and worried that my minimal understanding of mathematics would soon be discovered. I was automatically enrolled in the Operations Research Society and received monthly volumes filled with articles about subjects about which I knew virtually nothing. On the other hand, when the Project Management Institute was formed and I eventually became its vice president, my operations research colleagues didn't understand why project management would be such a big deal. Ironically, the Operations Research Society now counts fewer than 8,000 members worldwide, while the Project Management Institute has over 120,000.

The only thread that linked me to operations research was the systems approach. Since there was little perceived need for project management technologies at ADL, I looked for opportunities to apply the systems approach to my own field. In project management, everything starts with the work breakdown structure, and this turned out to be a much-needed tool in the professional work of the Company. Typically, when a new case team was formed to define and plan the approach to a particular problem, there were long discussions that failed to lead to a structured close. I found I was able to produce work breakdown structures for projects ranging from urban development in New York City to the implementation of a refinery in Kuwait by identifying all the elements of the project, their hierarchical relationships, and responsible organizations. Sometimes, I was asked to review a proposal that was already sent out to the client. I would quickly sketch out the work breakdown structure and often discover that a major part was either missing or had not been priced. This meant that much of my work turned out to be not for clients but for colleagues.

When the Department of Transportation was organized, the subject of traffic safety became its first focus. The automobile manufacturers also had concerns about the potential effectiveness of this activity and consequently sponsored a research project to determine the state of the art in traffic safety. Because of my demonstrated automotive interests, I became one of the core team members for the study with the primary responsibility for the driving aspects. This study took us on visits to all the major auto manufacturers in Detroit, their test tracks and research facilities. At times, the team members became victims of traffic safety concerns themselves. After a team visit to Detroit, we hailed a taxi to take us back to the airport. The driver seemed uncertain of the way and had to stop several times to ask for directions. It was only when he finally got on the highway that we noticed he was weaving all over the road. In fact, he was drunk. We quickly discussed whether we should drop this cab and look for another one, but were afraid we might miss our flight. Fortunately, the nation's first traffic safety team crossed their fingers and reached the airport safely.

The study did, however, result in an accident that left a permanent mark. At its successful conclusion, the National Safety Council awarded us a prize that included several thousand dollars. ADL management did not know how to spread this money around. After much discussion, it was decided to order customized desk clocks for each member of the team and to hold a cocktail party at which the clocks would be awarded. As it turned out, there were some slight differences from one clock to another. After the prizes were handed out, the recipients were curious to compare the variations in their prizes. My section head lifted his clock up to show it to me at the same instant as I was bending down to have a closer look at it. As a result, his clock collided with my front tooth, leaving a chip. In my application for workers compensation, I listed the reason for the damage as collision with a traffic safety prize.

The changing environment

In the 1970s, the environment at ADL began to change. Divisions and sections were being formed within the principal practice areas, and section heads were charged with profitability of their operations. This had an effect on the formation of case teams and carrying out client assignments. In the past, an open market system had prevailed. When a case leader was assigned, he would look throughout the organization for the people that would be the best qualified to solve the problem. It was not unusual for the Company chairman to work on a case under a junior staff member. When the division and section heads were made accountable for the billability of all the personnel in their own area pressure was put on the case leaders to keep work within the section. This meant that it was no longer possible to draw on the most qualified individuals in the Company and often resulted in less than the optimum case team. Even more importantly, it created difficulties for the working cooperation between R&D and management consulting units.

The ADL corporate culture that fostered and encouraged interaction between the practitioners of diverse disciplines enabled the consultants to solve problems that would have baffled many competitors. An example was the investigative work in the early nineties for a company specializing in the recovery of silver values from jewelry and other silver-containing scrap.

The company had recently established a West coast branch intended to recover silver from scrap generated by local defense contractors. The first batch of scrap from a new client, supplied in 50-gallon stainless steel drums, had been found to contain an unexpected black sludge. After the silver recovery process, the tray containing the black sludge had been left to dry in an open courtyard where it later exploded killing a nearby workman. The Los Angeles bomb squad attributed the explosion to substances believed to have been formed during the course of the silver recovery operation.

After taking on the case, ADL examined the explosion residues and found that the black sludge contained metallic titanium in the form of exceedingly thin flakes. Thermo chemical calculations showed that a reaction between metallic titanium and one of the substances generated in the silver recovery process could release energy equivalent to that of high explosives. ADL was, however, at a loss to understand the presence of the titanium.

After gaining access to the facility from which the client had received the waste solution, the consultants took samples one of which contained the black sludge. After drying, this material was found to contain exceedingly thin flakes of metallic titanium that proved to be violently explosive. Still, the investigative team could not explain the origins of the titanium.

While this study was under way, another group of ADLers was operating a facility to study the application of vacuum evaporated metallic coatings to various substrates. When the two groups compared notes, they noted that a thin coating of vacuum-evaporated titanium was routinely used as a primer before applying the silver coating to glass mirrors. The consultants concluded that since titanium was not attacked by the nitric acid used in periodic cleanup of the client's vacuum application apparatus, it formed the black sludge found in the waste solution. As the sludge went through the silver recovery process, it picked up the substance that would render it highly explosive.

Gradually the emerging political aspects also left an imprint on the quality and cost of the work for clients. ADL was known for industry specialists who kept up-to-date with their business areas but these positions were pretty much eliminated in the later days. At the same time, while the Company got rave reviews on its technological work, its management consulting work did not always match the quality expectations. There were numerous instances when the management consulting jobs did not produce the expected results and the client could have asked for the return of his money.

The compensation maze

Compared with the employees of other similar companies, ADLers had modest salaries. It was through profit sharing and various incentive programs that wealth was accumulated. Participation in the Memorial Drive Trust (MDT) provided a windfall through investment in such fast-growing companies as Continental Cablevision.

Already in the thirties, an entity known as Arthur D. Little Associates was used to channel a share of the profits to key senior employees. The remuneration schemes changed over time, but during the growth period, starting in the sixties, everybody shared in the Company's performance. The regular paycheck was reduced by 25%. This amount was paid out contingent on a planned performance factor that was set for each quarter. At the end of the quarter, the withheld portion of the paycheck was multiplied by the actual performance factor reflecting the Company's operating results. Most of the time, this factor was above 1.0 and resulted in raising the employee income. Some quarters, however, ended with a loss, and the employees received less than their stated salaries. ADL also established a Senior Participant group as a means of profit sharing for selected managers. The percentage of their salary indexed by the performance factor was higher and they could also receive additional discretionary payments.

Also during the sixties, it was possible to share the write-in[3] from a case that was completed below budget. This had a down side since some sections dealing primarily with technological issues could draw on work that had been done previously and produce significant write-ins that could be distributed to the participants. Another bone of contention was the informal method whereby section heads allocated the write-ins to the case participants. Some consultants who felt they had contributed to a case, never benefited from the write-in.

Those staff members who were on long-term assignments abroad received from various overseas allowances and tax benefits. In some instances, this could result in doubling the basic salary. Some money was also spread around in the form of Presidential awards. They were given to case leaders and others who had brought in valuable cases or had successfully completed difficult ones.

---

[3] A write-in is the extra profit resulting from a fixed price contract whose execution costs less than the hours billed against it.

A sales credit system was introduced in the late eighties. The idea was to reflect the true cost of business development and provide an accurate means of tracking responsibility for sales around the Company. A percentage estimate would be made of the contribution the case leader and other staff members had made in bringing in a case. The evaluations were not fully quantifiable and the results did not have a direct relationship to remuneration, but they where considered as part of the performance evaluation along with billability and other factors.

After establishment of a directorate system in 1989, the contingent portion of the paycheck was modified and specific incentives were set for staff members at each career stage level. Variable compensation was paid out partly on the basis of corporate performance and partly on the performance of directorates. Payment to the directorate staff was based on individual performance relative to standards for an individual's career level. At some management levels, as much as fifty percent of the salary was subject to the incentive formula, leading to occasional large bonuses for some of the directors.[4]

In the mid-nineties, as the ADL stock increased in value to the point where it was split, all top managers were required to purchase ADL shares. In addition, the current employee portion of the MDT retirement trust was funded primarily with ADL stock. This was well received as long as the value of the stock increased, but it later resulted in great losses.

---

[4] The Management Consulting directors were paid much more than Environmental and Technology directors leading to conflicts and raising the question who contributed most to the bottom line.

CHAPTER 4

Making It Go

At the end of an outstanding presentation to a client, the case leader mentioned that he had overrun the case by a few thousand dollars. The client was so impressed by the results that he immediately made out a check for the difference and the case leader took it back with him to Cambridge. Senior Vice President Reid Weedon startled him by demanding that the check be returned. He pointed out that ADL was serious when a proposal stated that the charges would not exceed a specified amount without a prior agreement. "If we had asked for the extra funds before the case was completed, we would have been happy to accept the money."

ADL's services were offered on a client-consultant basis to a diverse group of clients in many parts of the world. These included industrial, commercial, and service corporations, national, state, and local governments, trade associations, and non-profit institutions. For many years, generating new business was not a problem, and ADL had no need for a marketing or sales organization. Each day, as about twenty leads and requests for proposals came in, Karl Klaussen, the contracting officer, called on his small "network of boys" to discuss significant leads and decide which ones ADL would bid on and who would be responsible for each of them.

As the organization grew and became more complex, some staff members, particularly women who often felt they were in a secondary position, objected to the arbitrary way in which new cases were assigned. There was also an impression that some people never got the leads for which they were qualified, that instead they went to the friends of the management. The establishment of the Lead

Management Committee (LMC) was supposed to respond to this problem, but it never worked to everyone's satisfaction.

As business requirements evolved, some leads presented new problems because they did not fit into the existing experience. Such leads often were referred to the Operations Research section. Many leads required a quick response, so that by the time the LMC met, all they could do was to review the proposed staff assignments. For example, when a request came in to help set up the Massachusetts lottery, some LMC members wanted to reject it outright because they felt gambling was immoral. A recently hired marketing manager insisted that if ADL would not bid on it, somebody else would. In the end, a small team was put together, a proposal was written, and the contract was won.

Aside from key management personnel, the LMC included several staff members who were rotated in and out at certain intervals. Theoretically, this gave everybody a chance to participate in the lead assignment process. The committee also included members from the technology area although they often felt they did not hold their own against the management types.

The LMC identified the professional staff members most likely to be able to define and carry out a project and prepare a proposal. ADL prepared about 3000 proposals each year with approximately one half accepted by the client. When the client accepted the proposal, a case team was formed to fit the requirements of the particular assignment. The case team normally consisted of the people who defined the project and prepared the proposal.

Personal contact was the most important means of lead generation. Excellent professional performance on cases was a close second and was recognized as essential if personal contacts were to be productive over a period of time. Many of the lead generation techniques, such as professional papers, speeches, promotion, and public relations were also effective.

Sometimes the decisions of the LMC could be overruled. For example, when an opportunity arose to study the effectiveness of the telephone services provided by AT&T, the LMC did not want to take on the task because AT&T was a good friend of the Company and the results of the study could have proved to be unfavorable. The attitude was that certain big companies were friends and ADL should stay away from anything that might displease them. However, General Gavin who was Chairman at the time exclaimed, "AT&T does not control us" and supported the project.

Government work was often discouraged because it was not considered profitable and was not within the tradition of ADL. At one point, some ADLers started to explore opportunities with the Commonwealth of Massachusetts, which spent about $20 million a year on consultants. In this instance, senior management did not support the effort, as they did not want to have anything to do with the "Democrats of South Boston."

Staff members sometimes felt it was desirable to generate work only for themselves and for those for whom they were directly responsible. They felt a tremendous pressure to be billable at least to the levels set for their profit center but sensed little reward for finding work for people outside their organizational unit. When the Company became more structured in the eighties and nineties, there was increased management pressure to do all the work within the sections.

In some situations, no matter how tempting they were, the best tactic was not to sell at all. It was generally felt that if no one wanted to work on a job, it was only fair to say so at the outset. When ADL hired a marketing person in the late '70s, he was shocked to discover that after much effort in generating a prospect, a staff member could simply turn it down. At times, there was a good reason to refuse a client from the very beginning. For example, the prospect might be looking for a scapegoat to endorse his position, and would have no interest in independent findings. A client had to understand that ADL would say what the consultants honestly believed on the basis of a competent study, and that it would not rubber stamp its report. On the other hand, there was always the chance that the report would give the results desired by the client.

For example, General Dynamics engaged ADL to review the shipbuilding process of one of its subsidiaries. The case team found some serious problems and duly presented its recommendations. The Chairman of the corporation did not show any interest in the report's conclusions. He was simply looking for a justification to fire the division president and he had gotten it.

In another instance, the attorneys for Senator Ted Kennedy called ADL after his passenger drowned in the Chappaquidick bridge accident to determine how long it takes for a car to submerge after falling from the unlucky bridge. The call was taken by a staffer who had recently completed a study on traffic safety. Aside from the fact that he was a Republican and did not want to help the embattled senator, he believed there were too many variables to come up with meaningful results and he turned the lead down. The attorneys called again and this time were connected to somebody in the Engineering Division who was willing to take on the case.

Sometimes, it seemed wise to think twice about a prospect who, although willing to pay for the work, in fact posed a problem for which the solution had no real value to society. In circumstances where it appeared that there was a high likelihood that the issue of a study might be one simple result, the consultant often proposed a brief initial study to verify that conjecture quickly and inexpensively.

Although ADL was careful not to take on assignments that could be construed as a conflict of interest, sometimes the lines were not clearly drawn. For example, the Company found itself investigated for a conflict of interest when it developed EPA guidelines for pollution control at the same time that it was working for major chemical companies. A Congressional committee subpoenaed materials where they found a statement made by a junior staff member that the EPA case should present an opportunity for more business. The congressmen called for an explanation.

On the day before ADL was to appear in Washington, its top executives held a strategy meeting. It was noted that one of the staff members in the section had recently died. As a result, it was decided that the Commitee would be informed that he was the only person who had known all the details about the potential conflict. ADL would give some excuses and get off the hook.

To save money, the staff members who were to appear before the Committee were advised to fly in economy class and to not stay overnight. Despite this advice, they took the plane the night before so as to get a good night's sleep. Much to their mutual surprise, they found the executives on the same flight—in first class.

Getting the work done

ADL's organization could be described in two ways. One, the common organization chart, would display a more or less traditional triangle from trustees and directors through the president and vice presidents, division and section heads. In the other, the real organization, the case leader in charge of the case was a senior representative of ADL to the client, and had responsibility and authority to use the resources of the Company for the benefit of his client. Surprisingly enough the senior management honestly believed in this organization structure and was willing to back it up. There was a famous case in which a junior staff member was the case leader on one of the first technical audits. As the most qualified team for this assignment, he chose the President of ADL and three vice presidents.

In line with the Company's instinct that good case leaders are more important than administrators, for a long time there were few formal titles in the Company compared with most consulting firms and service organizations. Nevertheless, by 1985 the Company had 66 vice presidents.

The ADL structure was that of a collection of entrepreneurs who subcontracted work to each other. The formation of case teams exemplified the creation of *ad hoc* centers of authority and the pattern of casework demonstrated the belief in the supreme value of personal contact. Three kinds of personal contact were considered to be important: those with other ADLers to acquire knowledge and ideas, those with outsiders sharing the same purpose, and those with customers to generate business. The most important qualification for a consultant was the skill to develop and use contacts of all three kinds.

These relationships were encouraged and exploited in a number of ways. Although ADLers spent much time on travel, the concentration of staff at Cambridge was intended to facilitate the interchange of knowledge and ideas. The organization was deliberately kept open with few formal channels. Recruitment of case teams by the case entrepreneur and member's freedom to seek and refuse membership indicated a belief in the superior judgment of the man on the spot. The preference for relatively large case teams and for simultaneous work on several cases was further evidence of the desire to facilitate and make use of interpersonal exchanges. Working on several cases at the same time made it easier to plan continuous employment and to find billable time somewhere else if a case was held up.

As in any organization, there were a few people who preferred to work alone rather than in teams. Usually, these were experts who had established reputation before they joined ADL and had brought with them a wide circle of profitable clients. Unless they had these characteristics, they found themselves limited in their advancement opportunities and often left.

ADLers often went out of their way to please good clients. When the executive of a Brazilian oil company visited Cambridge and brought along his wife, arrangements were made to show her around Boston. Since the public relations people not were willing to help, the task was assigned to the case leader's secretary.

The executive's wife was a young and gracious society matron from a distinguished and powerful Rio de Janeiro family. Her family owned the biggest newspaper and her grandfather had been responsible for the planning and construction of the defense works at the entrance to the harbor. Instead of wanting to see the highlights of Boston, she expressed an interest in politics.

With nothing better in mind, the secretary took the visitor for a tour of the State House. During the tour, they ran into a politician with whom the secretary had previously worked and the ADLer introduced him to the guest. Within minutes, somebody appeared to ask if the ladies would like to meet the Secretary of State. Other invitations followed, the visit developing into a grand tour of the state administrative hierarchy. Shortly before noon, a page from the Governor's office appeared with an invitation to visit the Governor immediately after lunch. The Governor was gracious in meeting a distinguished guest from a friendly South American ally. The visitor was equally gracious. The state photographer was called in to record the historic event. The Governor sent a note to the General court, which was in session, asking if they too would be interested in meeting the distinguished guest. The Court called for a recess to permit its members to chat with the guest.

The client seemed to be blown away by his wife's experiences. He said he got the impression that ADL wielded such political clout as to permit shutting down the Massachusetts state government on short notice.

From time to time, ADL tried to identify areas in which they were weak and consciously tried to recruit personnel for those areas. Such attempts were rarely successful because the new activities did not get adequate management support. On the other hand, from time to time ADL hired someone who had a burning desire to work on a problem that ADL had never considered before. For example, a new staff member who came up with the concept of flavor profiles not only helped to solve an important problem for the food industry, but also attracted to the Company other people who had the competence and a desire to do something new and exciting. ADL's flavor laboratory eventually became a nationally known resource for companies in the food and beverage industry.

Staff communications

The Company cafeteria was used as an important tool for comunication. While some staff members preferred to sit with their colleagues, others made it a point to sit with different people each day. CEO John Magee often came in and joined one of the groups. In the '60s and '70s, the cafeteria was the location for other notable events. This was the era of serious drinking and whenever an ADLer had a significant anniversary or was leaving the company there was a major cocktail party after work. Martinis were the consumed, speeches were made, and presents were handed out.

Unlike the employees of some other companies at the time, ADLers did nor take formal coffee breaks. Some secretaries brewed their own coffee while others fetched it from the cafeteria. An exception during the sixties was the coffee break practiced in a section of a building that was closed off for secret government work. A few informal minutes spent here gave staff members an opportunity to exchange ideas outside the scope of work. Also, on Sunday afternoons, the head of the Operations Research section held an open house where staff members and their spouses could drop in to have a few drinks and discuss anything from case work to beagles (his wife was breeding them).

One of the most unusual institutions was the late afternoon meeting. Almost every day, some staff member scheduled a 4 p.m. meeting and invited five or six others. The purpose of the meeting that usually lasted two or three hours was to discuss an aspect of an ongoing case, a proposed marketing approach, or simply to get ideas from other staff members on solving a problem. Since these meetings went beyond the 5 p.m. closing time, the invitees needed special inducement to attend. This materialized exactly at 5 p.m. when the doors would open and a facilities person would roll in a cart with drinks, cheese and crackers. Initially, everybody would ignore it. Gradually one or two of the more courageous would get up and pour a martini. Eventually, everyone would help themselves. These meetings were so popular that the conference rooms had to be reserved far in advance.

Resumes and qualifications

An important part of marketing in any consulting company is the trove of Company experiences and staff resumes. For many years, assembly of such valuable information was not well organized. There was no guidance given as to how to prepare the resume for a particular client and the best one could do was to look at the resumes of other staff members.

A proposal generally included a description of pertinent work done by the Company and the resumes of the staff members who were assigned to the task. Eventually collections of related experience were assembled and used in preparing proposals. What was misleading here was that the client was given the impression that all of the described capabilities were available at the Company. In actuality, many of the cases described the work of staff members who no longer worked at the Company. Those who had replaced them often could not match their experience and skills.

The cost of doing business

An invoice from consultants consisted of two parts: a charge for professional services and expenses, each shown separately. ADL had a firm policy not to quote charges in terms of daily rates, or to break out the charges on invoices. At one point ADL started to itemize the invoice, but soon ran into too much difficulty with clients who tried to save money by asking that the higher-paid staff members spend less time on the case. The case leader was responsible for the quality of the work, and ADL management felt strongly that he should have the flexibility to make use of any resource he had available to get the right solution within the authorized budget.

Sometimes, if the client insisted, ADL would agree to the appointment of a mutually acceptable accounting firm. It would have access to such records as necessary to ascertain and certify that charges were based on hours and rates that did not exceed those charged by other commercial clients for similar services and would insure that expenses were properly chargeable to the contract. It was understood that the cost of such an audit would be paid for by the client.

In the proposal, expenses were usually expressed as a percentage of the professional charges, but it was often hard to predict what the actual expenses would be. Most clients were not aware that ADL added a ten percent surcharge to all expense items from lunches to first-class airline tickets. This charge was supposed to contribute to the cost of handling the expense items, although this was already included in the overhead rate reflected in professional fees.

In one case, the client learned about the surcharge and justifiably became quite upset. After some negotiation, he agreed to pay a fixed charge for the expenses rather than actuals plus the surcharge. As it turned out, the consultants were able to keep their expenses to a minimum, and the change cost the client more than originally proposed.

After each trip, the consultants turned in an expense report itemizing all they had spent on behalf of the client. This was reviewed and approved by a supervisor. Again, some clients never suspected what the charges included. If asked out to dinner, many would assume that it was at ADL's expense. Actually, it was charged to the case and subject to the ten percent surcharge. Some of the costs of frequent travel were incurred over time and could not be properly reflected on the expense account. For example, suitcases were not built as strongly as they are now, and sometimes had to be replaced after two or three trips. When questioned about this by a frustrated consultant, the section head confessed that he routinely added $10 to each of his weekly expense accounts. Over time, this gave him the funds to buy a new suitcase.

The greatest use of expense accounts, however, was the lunch. One consultant recalls that when he first joined ADL, he was given a list of consultant names and told to invite them to lunch so that they could get to know him and invite him to work on their cases. Of course, the costs of such lunches were covered by the Company or, more likely, by the client whose case came up during the conversation.

In the '60s, the most popular lunch place for ADLers was the restaurant Fantasia. Located less than a mile from the Cambridge headquarters, the restaurant had an entire room that was generally populated by ADL consultants. The decor of the restaurant, designed by a Latvian architect from New York, was reminiscent of the '30s. With martinis and oysters on half-shell as the most popular items on the menu, it provided a sharp contrast to the ADL facility where no alcohol was served before 5 o'clock.

The hardest drinkers were the engineers who worked with clients in the oil industry. Lunches usually lasted two to three hours and required two or three martinis. One of the seasoned consultants was known for gulping his first martini and calling for the waitress to bring him the other half of the drink. For somebody not used to these libations, the remaining afternoon would be wasted.

Over time, these practices evolved along with changes in the society. The Fantasia restaurant was raized to make room for an office complex and more people restricted their lunches to in-house facilities. If a very special client needed to be entertained, one could engage the resources of ADL's Food and Flavor section that would prepare a gourmet meal that included wine in their "Oak Leaf Room." As might be expected, a case number to charge the time and expense was necessary.

Cost control

Looking for additional sources of income, somebody in accounting came up with the idea to confiscate the frequent flyer miles that staff members were accumulating. While there was precedent for this in some other companies, it did not fly very well at ADL. Some ADLers circulated a memo asking their colleagues to also turn in to the

Company all the little paper umbrellas they got with their drinks when traveling. Soon thereafter, the idea of taking employee frequent flyer miles was dropped.

Getting professionals to stay within tight budgets is not an easy task, and ADL was not very good at enforcing this policy. Since each case was unique and no comparable records were kept when they were similar, each case budget had to start from scratch. The case leader estimated the hours needed to do the job, the section head reviewed it and the financial people priced it out according to the billing rates that were kept confidential.

Consulting firms often have to finance a significant amount of receivables, and during a period of high interest rates this presented a cash flow problem for ADL. To alleviate it, a 10% surcharge on expenses was introduced. Some people misinterpreted the rationale for this new policy and took to flying first-class to make more money for the company through the surcharge.

Each section had a business manager but the functions they performed varied from one to another. Some were only clerks who kept numbers while others handled lead assignment; reviewed proposals and arranged interviews for new candidates. In such a position, they had a lot of hidden power and the opportunity to learn a lot about the styles of the case  leaders. Until the seventies, ADL had no formal human resources function. It did not want one, as that would have caused standardization of pay rates and other incentives.

Many staff members could be described as "artists" who aspired to doing the best job possible for the client. This meant that case budgets were overrun more frequently than underrun. If extra funds were left near the completion of a case, they were often used to improve the product still further. This made it difficult for the section heads whose performance rating was affected by overruns.

A category of work particularly susceptible to overruns was the multi-client study. ADL would make a proposal to a number of companies to study a particular subject such as the potash market in the world, and divide the cost among them to come up with a fixed price. Quite often the clients suggested refinements in the study that were accepted by the case leader, but also increased the cost. Other expenses, such as for travel, also were likely to exceed estimates. As a result, the budgets for multi-client studies were often exhausted long before the work was completed. As a solution, the case leader would hit the road to try to line up more clients for the product. Fortunately for ADL, they succeeded in most cases.

ADL never knew how successful it had been in terms of money because the budgeting and cost accounting system did not allow for follow-up on past work. Some cases ended with a surplus and resulted in write-ins but because of the policy not to exceed a quoted price, others cost more than was paid by the client. Even if consultants working on their own time absorbed the extra effort, such information on past cases would have been very useful for pricing similar bids. This procedure was improved in later years but never worked very effectively.

Time card management

The product of a consulting business is time and the key to profits is billability. One of the reasons lawyers have a bad image is that some of them charge the client what he can bear, at times with the result that a lawyer charges more time than the hours in a day. This is not so likely in the consulting business. While most ADL contracts included a clause that similar work had been done in the past and the current proposal might include additional charges for this benefit, it was just as likely that more hours would be spent on the job than was priced into the contract. Usually, this meant the client got something for nothing.

ADLers were usually expected to be billable at least 72 % of the time.[1] Some new employees did not reach this goal, but others consistently reported 95 % or higher billability. When a staff member proved to be this valuable, the section head could add a surcharge to his billing rate and thus generate side income that could be used for marketing, education or other purposes.

For many years, ADL had a very loose timekeeping system. In the fifties, some case leaders took advantage of it by overcharging and then filing revisions the following week. This made both their cases and their billability look good, since by the time the system caught up with the changes, all the reports had been acted on and filed away.

Each staff member turned in a time card on Thursdays with an estimate of the work he or she anticipated doing on Friday so as to come up with a total of forty hours. The section heads collected these time cards and often made some changes. For example, if a case was being overrun and risked a loss of profit, a section head might borrow time from another case that had ample budget. In addition, he would allocate his own free time to any cases where budget permitted it. One section head simply charged an hour a week to every case that came across his desk. As a result, some case leaders were shortchanged and had to do with smaller budgets than initially planned. At times, this resulted in less qualitative work.

While this timekeeping method had the effect of lifting the section's billability, it had several weaknesses. First, since some people worked on a number of cases and their time was not always accounted for during the week, errors were likely. Second, it was not always

---

[1] The billability targets for some senior people were higher, but at the same time, their billing rates were as high as double the regular rates. Thus, a senior level consultant may have actually needed only 36% billability to reach a given income target.

possible to predict on Thursday which cases would require attention on Friday. While in theory it was possible to turn in revisions, they were seldom made. More frequently, adjustments were made in the subsequent week's timecard—if one could remember it. Third, since the timecards accounted for only forty hours, they did not properly reflect the actual time spent on a client's behalf. From a project management viewpoint, such information would have been useful for estimating and budgeting of similar cases in the future.

Management had always pushed for recording the weekly hours exceeding 40, but this practice was not followed by many case leaders who wanted to save their case budget in case it took longer than estimated. It was clear that if they could show a surplus at the completion, they might also be able to share in the write-in.

Another, even more serious weakness in the timekeeping system was the fact that it did not reflect the time devoted to marketing. Billability was key, but since ADL did not have a marketing department until the '80s, each staff member was expected to do his own selling. If the visit to a client took half-a-day, it made sense not to grab the next plane home, but rather visit other potential clients in that city and charge the entire day to the case. Sections could set up marketing budgets against which staff members could charge their time, but since this counted against the sections billability and affected the section head's compensation, it was not widely practiced. Staff members would most likely charge the marketing time to a large case that had plenty of budget. Aside from the question of whether this was fair to the clients, it distorted the cost history of the case.

A question that bothered many consultants was how to deal with overtime and hours spent on travel. It was an easy decision on day trips that could be charged to a particular client. Frequently, client visits lasted several days and meetings often ran late into the night. Although the client usually thought he got the extra time for nothing, the consultant may have charged the overtime on the day after he returned back home.

The real goldmine for freely billable hours came with some government contracts. Since they usually dealt with scientific subjects, the administrative side was seen as a nuisance both by the client and the consultants. Nevertheless, the government required that a certain percentage of the contract amount be devoted to the preparation and submission of administrative reports. With some experience, it was possible to complete the reports in a fraction of the time that was budgeted for it. The balance could be painlessly used for some marketing activity.

From time to time, the Defense Contracting Agency performed "floor checks" to audit time cards. Sometime in the nineties they found enough problems to require that the timekeeping system be changed in keeping with accepted practices—that time be recorded each day and reported at the end of the week instead of midweek.

The system was changed requiring that timecards be filled out each day. To comply with Massachusetts tax rules, consultants were also supposed to indicate in which state the charges were incurred. The federal government required that the first 40 hours of each week be reported as regular, and any others as overtime for which they would not pay. Previously, the "best 40 hours" had been recorded first and the government was billed for all the hours spent on its behalf. Now, it became difficult to schedule time so as not to push the government hours beyond any private sector hours and make them non-billable.

Closely related to timekeeping was the issue of overhead distribution. Clearly, it was more expensive to maintain a laboratory than to cover the cost of a group of traveling consultants. Also, since the same staff members would be working on government as well as private sector assignments, it was difficult to implement a method that would accurately reflect the costs of each. Following the ADL bankruptcy, one of the outstanding claims was from a whistleblower who accused the Company of falsifying overhead rates on government contracts. The idea was that different rates should have been charged for different sections of the Company. ADL had decided that this was too difficult to do. By the time of the bankruptcy, this potential claim had grown with interest and penalties to more than $100 million.

CHAPTER 5

Brick and Mortar

The professonal staff is the key asset of a consulting company. When consultants are not visiting client sites, however, they need a quiet place to work, think, prepare reports, and meet with case team members and other colleagues. Anyone who has visited one of the nation's principal consulting firms will attest to the striking overall architecture and the meticulous order of their facilities, both intentionally designed to impress the potential client. Common wisdom would have it that creating the proper environment conveys a sense of success.

At ADL, this was different. Until the last decade when the reception area was finally redesigned, the visitor was immediately struck by the austere concrete block buildings and the modesty of the offices. ADLers gave the impression of being concerned with the client's problems, not the size of their own desk or chair. At one time, even former CEO General Gavin received visitors in an obscure office that had heating pipes running along the walls. Former Board chairman Robert Mueller occupied another windowless office not much larger than a walk-in closet.

It all started in 1916 when Dr. Little issued $150,000 of new stock in the Company and used the proceeds to buy land and construct a building at 30 Charles River Road in Cambridge. This was just around the corner from MIT's new location in an area soon known as *Research Row*. While Dr. Little called it a *research palace*, others were known to call it *Little's folly*. Although the name of the thoroughfare was changed to Memorial Drive after the war, Dr. Little stubbornly used the Charles River Road address until he died. The building was designated as a National Historic Site by the Department of Interior in 1977 in recognition of its importance as the birthplace of industrial research. At the time of ADL's demise in 2002, this original site was taken over by MIT.

Most people associate ADL with its more recent Cambridge location at Acorn Park. The cornerstone for the first building on this site was laid on November 17, 1953. At that time, it was thought to be one of the most modern research laboratories in the United States. After an impressive ceremony that was attended by various dignitaries, the 9-year-old grandnephew of the late Dr. Little, and the four-year old grandchildren of Dr. Earl Stevenson, then President of ADL, participated in a tree planting ceremony. The presence of the children and the planting symbolized the theme "Dedicated to Tomorrow."

Enclosed in the cornerstone were a number of articles depicting significant ADL contributions to industrial progress. These included a 399 page report on the industrial opportunities in New England, a sun-baked mud brick developed especially for Egypt, a commercial version of algae that was intended to alleviate the shortage of food in the world, and a vial of distilled water made from seawater using a still designed and developed at ADL. It also included an acorn, the emblem of the Company selected by Dr. Little himself along with the notation "Scatter acorns that oaks may grow." The final items were a sample of monosodium glutamate that was studied by ADL before its introduction in the United States and a description of the ADL Collins Helium Cryostat that had been used in testing the fusion bomb.

Just ten years later, the Acorn Park facility was nothing to be proud of. Built simply with cinderblocks for inside walls, the standard size offices were so small they could barely accom- modate a desk and two chairs. Because it was fairly easy to rip out the cinderblock walls, section heads and their favorites managed to get double size offices. Division heads were awarded even more space.

Unlike many other companies that enforced a uniform decor and limited the extent to which employees could change the look of their offices, ADL imposed no restrictions. As a consequence many staff members kept plants, oriental carpets or their favorite pieces of furniture in their offices. One electronics expert outfitted his office like an airport control tower with all sorts of automated gadgets and dials. A marketing manager furnished her office with modernistic stainless steel furniture.

After joining ADL I had to put up with one of the very small offices for a number of years. At one point, I hosted a five-man German delegation including a colonel in full uniform in my office. As other staff members came in to make presentations, the guests were stuffed into the office so closely there was hardly any room for the presenter. Not wanting to leave the VIPs with the impression that I had an exceptionally small office, I made a point of taking them down the hall, carefully avoiding the larger offices, to introduce them to Ted Withington. He had written a number of books on data processing and was internationally known, but best of all, his office was just as small as mine. Nevertheless, for years afterwards whenever I ran into one of the delegates, they laughingly reminded me of the embarrassing event.

Eventually I came up with a way to get a larger office. Since my cases often involved working with multiple project management charts, I asked that a floor-to-ceiling particleboard be installed to display them. Nobody could question my need for it, and since this required more room than the standard office allowed, they finally found me a larger one.

As in any dynamic organization, ADL staffers were accustomed to moving to other buildings within Acorn Park or even to other locations, such as Burlington, Massachusetts. These were the occasions when political power plays were often necessary to secure the best offices. It was considered particularly desirable to be located near the section head's office, as that gave opportunities for casual discussion and, quite possibly, the first crack at an interesting case.

It seems that ADL was always ahead of it's time in its approach to problem solving. A serious facilities challenge emerged when a male staff member, after a brief absence, returned to work as a woman. His male colleagues did not want to see him in the men's room, and the women did not embrace him/her into theirs. After studying the rules for equal opportunity, the Company designated a separate toilet just for him/her.

For many decades, a green door blocked off the top floor of the building housing technology laboratories. This was the site of a secret Government project that required a high-level security clearance. In view of the secrecy, there were few rumors about the nature of the project, and many staff members did not even know about the existence of the green door. Managers or anyone else who knew the facts still refuse to talk about it. Some believe that revenue from the project was not even shown on the books or, at least, was hidden under another subject. Others suggest that the mysterious project never ended, and the green door may still be in existence.

In 1983, ADL set up a high-security laboratory at Acorn Park to accommodate a military contract for researching chemical nerve agents. Since the research involved some of the most deadly chemicals known to man, quite a few ADLers objected to this work. Others rationalized that the compounds to be studied were intended as temporary disabling agents and would not inflict permanent injury. The ADL public relations people let the word out to the conservative population of Cambridge and caused a public uproar. Local opposition groups formed a coalition called Toxic Alert. At first, ADL discounted the importance of the coalition, and then held meetings with them. The public relations efforts did not have much success, and the project was dropped after its leader died in a scuba diving accident that some viewed with suspicion.

Another embarrassing situation arose when an ADL researcher acquired small quantities of explosives, readily obtainable at the time, for legitimate casework. For some reason, the facilities personnel asked him to remove these explosives from a locked shed where he kept them. They also prohibited him from taking the explosives into his laboratory. Consequently, he made what seemed to him the best available decision, i.e. to store the carefully boxed and wrapped explosives in the open, near the ADL boundary fence. One night they disappeared, box and all, triggering a police investigation on the suspicion they might have fallen into the hands of terrorists. They were never found.

During the real estate boom in mid-eighties former staff member, Poly Vintiades, now a financier with Saudi funding, put together a package for redeveloping Acorn Park. His idea was to develop the area as a luxury mall and high-rises alongside the offices of ADL. The proposal died when ADL could not make up its mind whether to proceed in view of serious environmental problems related to the adjoining wetlands, as well as the emerging recession at that time.[1]

Faced with a growing need for facilities space, ADL also entertained the idea of constructing another office building at the Acorn Park site. It was postponed indefinitely in 1985 after writing off more than $1 million in architectural and engineering fees.

As the adjoining wetlands became more regulated each year, the value of the Acorn Park facility dropped. About 1997, ADL began to evaluate its office and laboratory space needs and explore alternatives for the Company. A decision seemed to have been reached when a suitable property was located at the intersection of nearby Routes 2 and 128. Negotiations were well under way with contractors when CEO Charlie LaMantia suddenly decided to drop the plan. He was reported to have said that he had too many things on his plate at the time.

Soon thereafter, suitable land became available in Weston where there was a possibility for ADL to build newer and more efficient offices. The idea was to tailor the Company's new headquarters to the needs of a consulting firm where many executives are out on the road most of the week.

"There is no use in building very expensive space if a person only occupies it one day a week," declared human resources director Sam Gallo. Because of their travel-heavy schedules, he wanted to assign some consultants to a different office each week. As it turned out, the Weston project also came to a premature end. Access by hundreds of cars to what had been an old quarry would have required costly road modifications, including a new exit from nearby Route 128.

In early 1999, representatives of a Philadelphia based real estate partnership, O'Neill Properties, approached ADL about the sale of Acorn Park and lease of space at their newly developed *Arsenal on the Charles* in Watertown. Since ADL was in a desperate need of a cash infusion, the offer sounded interesting. After several months of negotiations, Acorn Park was sold for $20 million. At the same time, ADL entered into a 20-year lease for more modern and efficient facilities in Watertown. Pictures of the new facility were displayed

---

[1] Another limiting factor for any expansion was the fact that ADL did not own part of the main parking lot.

throughout the Company cafeteria, and Charlie LaMantia joked that the only thing that was holding up the move was trying to figure out how to disassemble and reinstall Acorn Park's cinder block walls.

Curiously, the Board approved the sale without an independent valuation of the property. The facility was sold so cheaply that questions were raised as to whether some insiders had actually benefited from the transaction.[2] The trustees of the ESOP plan considered that the ADL Board had been grossly negligent in approving the sale and engaged a law firm to investigate. The issue was dropped when the lawyers concluded that, according to Massachusetts law, the only way to hold the directors accountable was to prove that they had personally benefited from the transaction.[3]

The $20 million obtained from the sale did not go very far, and with a tight cash flow, ADL once more had to relinquish plans for relocation. The move to Watertown was abandoned. With no other place to go, ADL was forced to lease back the Acorn Park space from its new owners. The Company paid dearly for this unfortunate turn of events.

After changing its mind about relocation, ADL was left with a long-term lease on about 360,000 square feet of office space at the Watertown development. At the time, real estate in Boston area was much in demand and, fortunately, ADL was able to sublease most of the space at a premium. However, as the technology business suddenly deflated, renters disappeared, and ADL was stuck with expensive lease payments. At the time of the bankruptcy, it owed $2.3 million for past due rent.

In the meantime, O'Neill Properties had sold the Watertown complex along with the ADL lease to Harvard University. With ADL unable to pay, the value of the property suffered, and Harvard filed a claim of about $30 million.

After the bankruptcy in 2001, the new owners of Acorn Park renamed it Cambridge Innovations Park. Thus, an important piece of the Arthur D. Little legacy was completely erased from the map.

---

[2] Three months after the sale, the property was appraised at $45 million, and it was then sold soon afterwards for $63 million. Under the Massachusetts bankruptcy law, O'Neill Properties was considered to have acquired the property under "fraudulent conveyance" and a suit was brought to recover the difference between the value of the property and the price paid.

[3] The Board could be still sued if it can be proven that they made a bad decision. This would be difficult, however, since it deals with judgment based on the available facts.

CHAPTER 6

On the Road

Two young ADL staff members traveled to Tulsa for a presentation to a major oil company. Upon arriving in Chicago, they found themselves in the middle of a storm and discovered that their connecting flight had been cancelled. They found a couple of free berths on an overnight train and then called to forewarn the client about the unexpected delay.

Early the next morning, somewhere in the middle of Kansas, the train conductor woke them up with the surprising news that they were to be picked up. After scrambling to collect their belongings, the ADLers were let off at an obscure railroad crossing right next to a shiny oil company plane that was waiting for them in the middle of a field.

Travel is an inescapable part of consulting. In 1984, ADL spent a total of $6 million on employee travel. It was said that the pulse of the Company's operations could be measured by just looking at the parking lot. If there were many open spaces, it meant business was good.

People sometimes did not want to tell colleagues where they were going since it might be a place somebody else regarded as his own territory. Occasionally, this led to embarrassing situations, particularly when two staff members arrived at a prospective client without knowing the other one was already there.

The best period for business travel was in the sixties. It was an era when many companies condoned first-class travel for cross-country and transcontinental business trips. In flight, champagne flowed freely and it was not unusual for the consultants to straggle off the airplane in Los Angeles or San Francisco in an exuberant mood. However, despite the pleasantries of travel, most consultants still preferred to be home, at least over the weekends. For those who were required to be away several weeks at a time, special accommodations were occasionally made whereby the consultants spouse would fly out with him on the next trip. After all, it was figured, it did not cost any more for the spouse to fly out than it cost for the consultant to fly back and forth for a weekend at home.

Perks aside, a former ADLer recalls that on his very first business trip to Greenville, North Carolina, he ended up by mistake in Greenville, South Carolina, some 500 miles away! Somehow, he managed to do what needed to get done and showed up back in Cambridge when expected. It turns out, however, that he did not tell anyone in Cambridge about this for nearly a year afterwards.

One ADLer remembers an even more extreme situation when he was suddenly asked to go to Brazil. The client had questioned the

qualifications of one of the consultants who was working on the design of computer resources for a teaching hospital and asked that somebody else be sent out. Once he had arrived in Brazil, however, the delegated staff member found he had nothing to contribute, but he had to stay there for four weeks because of a contractual requirement. Needless to say, he had a great time in Rio.

In the sixties, ADL gathered an excellent group of scientists, engineers, and mathematicians for a large Navy contract. The travel to client meetings in Washington was an experience by itself. One usually took the helicopter that either left directly from a pad at ADL or another site in the suburbs to the airport and back later in the same way. The flights to Washington were pleasant enough, but when the travel time was taken into account, very little time was left to spend with the client. On some occasions, an ADLer would arrive in Washington shortly before lunch only to be told that the client was too busy and that the consultant should come back the next day. If this was the case, the consultant might have lunch at a nice D.C. restaurant, walk a bit around Washington, and catch an early flight home. In the meantime, his time card would show a hundred percent billability.

Not all of the consultant travels were on commercial airlines. One of ADL's largest clients in Brazil was a construction company that had its own fleet of airplanes. Although they were well maintained and the pilots were competent, flying on them could be nerve wracking. An ADLer who worked on the project recalls flying back from a dam construction site as the only passenger on the two-engine plane. As they approached the state of Minas Gerais, storm clouds threatened and the ride became bumpy. When the sympathetic pilot noticed his passenger's discomfort, he put the plane on autopilot and joined him in the cabin with a bottle of scotch.

While the airplane was the most common travel method for consultants, an ADLer who was temporarily assigned to the London office got weary of flying and decided to experiment with crossing the ocean on the liner SS *France*. He liked the voyage so well that he became a frequent passenger at a time when steamship travel was on the way down. This paid off on one occasion when he was delayed on British roads on route to the port. He called the ship to tell them he was on his way. They answered they would wait for him. The road trip took much longer than expected, but the ship's passengers were never told the identity of the presumed VIP who had delayed their departure for several hours.

In the sixties, helicopter service was the preferred method for commuting between Acorn Park and Logan airport. Despite the proneness for accidents, most ADLers felt comfortable with this type of transportation. However, nothing could have prepared the staff member who experienced his wildest helicopter ride in Puerto Rico.

The Puerto Rican electric company had a tall downtown San Juan building with a heliport on top. The company helicopter was assigned to whisk a visiting ADL consultant to a nuclear plant that was being constructed on the other side of the island. The first thing the ADLer noticed was that the two-man helicopter did not have any doors. Held in his seat by a skimpy belt, he looked straight down to the fast disappearing ground. The next thing he noticed was a mountain range between San Juan and the other coast. The helicopter circled as it slowly gained height and soon reached an elevation usually reserved for airplanes. As the ADLer held tight to the seat, the pilot announced that because there were too many clouds on top of the mountains, he would have to return to San Juan. At first, the ADLer was relieved, as he really did not look forward to flying any higher. Just then, the pilot dipped the helicopter on its side and slid down the mountainside at breakneck speed. Once safely on the ground, the ADLer swore never to step into a helicopter again.

Sometimes, long airplane trips resulted in making acquaintances that benefited future business. Joe Voci tells of meeting a popular ADL executive at Logan Airport who was on the same flight. He was off to visit the London office while Joe planned to connect the next morning to Riyadh. After some two hours out on the flight, the captain reported that a mechanical problem had developed which demanded a return to Logan. The crew passed on the word to prepare for a rough landing: no drinks, pens out of pockets, heads to the knees, life preservers at the ready, straps secured, etc.

This scene of excitement caused a great deal of concern and confusion to a Saudi woman seated next to the ADL executive. The VIP took complete charge to calm her fears and help her through the landing ordeal, which, luckily, ended without a mishap. Back on the ground, the woman was now stressed out over the train of difficulties she might have to face alone in the event that her proposed travel schedule was interrupted: lodgings, baggage, communicating with her husband, plane reservations and such, all of which had to be attended to. The kindly executive pledged his full assistance, as well as that of Joe who was booked on the same Saudia Airlines flight through to Riyadh.

By the time the plane had finally taken off from Logan again, it was clear that they would miss the London connection with Saudia. This meant that the courteous offer of guardianship by the executive would now fall onto Joe's lap. At Heathrow, the executive parted with fair well wishes and instructions to Joe to look after the Saudi lady's comfort and her safe return home. Alone with a Saudi woman in London, Joe conjured up fearful thoughts of his own fate, not the least the image of "Chopping Block Square" and tons of stones.

Joe's first act was to secure a booking on the earliest carrier to anywhere in the Kingdom of Saudi Arabia. The airline arranged rooms for them at a large airport hotel where Joe prepared a fax to the woman's husband giving the new arrival schedule and the cause for the long delay.

The new flight left punctually next morning, but over Beirut, the first stop, the plane circled for a long time until the word was given that all planes were being diverted to other airports because of stubborn weather conditions. Cairo was chosen as the alternative-landing stop; the captain turned South-West, and prayed that there was still enough fuel for the ride. It now was late at night and somewhere over the Mediterranean the message was delivered for a third time during the journey that there would be a delay of some sort. The Cairo landing was now out of the question due to violent sand storms.

About that time, Joe could have used some help from the executive friend as his Saudi charge was again in a state of panic. After much commotion, they learned that there was enough thrust left in the engines to make it to Abu Dhabi, and the captain assured that all was clear for landing there. The weary travelers finally put their feet on the ground at Abu Dhabi at 2 a.m. on the second day of the venture. Because the airport services were down at that early morning hour, they were unable to book passage to Saudi ports until later in the morning.

Once inside the airport, there wasn't enough seating space to accommodate all the people who had arrived on the wayward flight. The weary Saudi lady rested on a bench with Joe on the floor until it was time to book the flights with Saudia. To be sure, Joe was first in line to make the reservations and fax the Saudi husband to hang on.

About noon, Joe boarded the Saudia flight with a happy-faced woman, now in full Saudi dress. When they parted in Riyadh, the Saudi woman overwhelmed Joe with many blessings, expressions of gratitude for his assistance, and with best wishes for the executive.

The follow-up to this incident took place a few months later at a leading Saudi ministry where a team of ADLers was busy with a proposal of considerable scope and duration. On the minister's side was a visitor, a prince of the royal family. During the session, the prince asked some ADLers if they knew Joe and the executive (always a risky question at this crucial stage of the negotiation!). They courteously admitted knowing the people in question. The prince then went on to tell of his wife's recent travel woes and of the ADLers assistance in escorting her safely home from Boston. He also remarked that he was pleased to have the Company's assistance at the ministry. There was little else needed by the Governor to strengthen ADL's relation with the ministry and pave the way for a prosperous business relationship.

Other acquaintances made on airplanes by ADLers were with stewardesses. Some kept lists of stewardess' addresses in various cities and shared them with their colleagues. A number of the girls were quite aggressive on their own, and particularly interested in pursuing those who flew first class. In one instance, a consultant found himself in a sticky situation when his wife discovered a letter addressed to him by an airline stewardess. She had looked up his name on the travel manifest and traced his address through a suburban telephone directory.

Even the virtuous effort of trying to keep women at a distance could sometimes backfire on traveling consultants. In one such situation, three ADLers were in Salt Lake City on an assignment for a copper mining company. The simple act of getting a relaxing drink after work was made difficult by the fact that there were no bars within the Salt Lake City limits at the time. They were told, however, that there was a bar located at the end of the main street. Still dressed in their business suits, the ADLers decided to walk to what, on the map, looked like a distance of four or five blocks. After having walked for about twenty minutes, however, they realized that these were particularly long blocks. The address they were looking for did not seem to be coming any closer.

As they stopped at a gas station to check in the phone book, a young man drove up in a red Austin Healey sports car and asked if he could help. "Yes, we are looking for the Top Hat bar." "Jump in," the man said. The ADLers hesitated for a minute, as the car was a two-seater and to accommodate all three people was no simple task. Somehow, they managed to squeeze into the small space, and, as the car pulled out into the street, it bottomed out with a bang. "You're going to hurt your car," one of the men ventured. "Don't worry," the young man answered, "it is not my car."

The prospect of finding themselves in the middle of Salt Lake City in an overloaded car that may have been stolen, on a road that was used as a drag strip by the local kids was not at all reassuring to the thirsty trio. They had already observed plenty of police cars hiding around corners and wondered if ADL would bail them out if they were picked up. The ride was long, they realized that they could have never made it on foot, and it felt even longer because of the anxiety. Fortunately, they made it safely to the Top Hat bar only to find that it served nothing better than a watery, three-percent beer.

CHAPTER 7

The Big Personalities

Managing the diverse pool of talent and intellect represented by the professional staff of a consulting company requires leadership, inspiration and vision. In the case of ADL, these requirements were not always met. For the first seventy years, the Company was highly regarded as a topnotch chemical laboratory dominated by technical talents. When operations research was added in the middle of the twenthieth century, and with it, new needs for new directions in management, the chemical engineers still remained firmly in control.

Whereas Dr. Little had a vision of his company as the leader in technology, Earl Stevenson, his successor, saw diversification in management consulting as the key to maximizing technological expertise. The people who followed Stevenson generally continued in the same vein but missed out on a single, vital strategy—using the technology base to carve a niche in the consulting business. With its deep understanding of research and development, ADL was better positioned than any of its competitors to solve business problems for technology companies.

The big change for ADL came in the sixties when the Company's past leadership in research and development became overshadowed by management consulting that emerged as an crucial area for the times. Fortunately for ADL, General James Gavin, who had come aboard in 1958, was able to provide the leadership, inspiration and vision needed in this period of transition. Unfortunately for ADL, he was called away to serve the U.S. Government and, in his absence, management of the Company was, once again, taken back by the technicians.

A key to the continuing success of ADL had been the fact that it offered a long leash to its consultants and did not require many top management approvals. The process of turning from a technology-oriented to a management consulting oriented company provided an opportunity to those staff members who were politically ori-ented and had big egos to climb over others and jockey for manage-ment positions. In this situation, turf battles were inevitable. Ironi-cally, the Board of Directors paid little attention to what was hap-pening within the Company.

Once the original top management line of chemical engineers (Dr. Little, Earl Stevenson and Ray Stevens) had left ADL, a small hand-ful of people dominated the evolution and eventual demise of the Company. This chapter gives a brief insight into what these people were like and the legacy they left behind.

General James Gavin

After the Second World War, General Gavin and Soviet Marshall Zhukov became acquainted as the commandants of their respective sectors of occupied Berlin. At one point during their Berlin tenure, Gavin decided to showcase the capabilities of his paratroopers to Zhukov and arranged for a demonstration in an athletic stadium. Zhukov, not to be outdone, ordered one of his officers to arrange for a similar Soviet demonstration a few weeks later.

Because the Soviets had no paratroopers at their disposal, they had little time to equip and train their soldiers for the event. When the Russian jump finally took place, the hapless Soviets landed any-where but in the stadium. Zhukov was outraged by this poor public display and unofficial rumor had it that he personally executed the officer in charge.

Years later, General Gavin, by then Chairman of ADL, and several of his colleagues flew to Moscow for an important business discussion.

Once again Gavin found himself face to face with Marshal Zhukov who had arranged a big dinner for the ADL delegation. After a few vodkas had been consumed, the two started reminiscing together about their Berlin years. Gavin took this inimate opportunity with the Soviet Marshall to find out the true story about the officer in charge of the paratrooper team. Zhukov paused for just a moment after Gavin's question and responded, "You've already heard it."

General Gavin originally gained fame as a paratroop leader in Europe during the Second World War. He resigned from the military after thirty-three years of service because he disagreed with the emerging doctrine of solving conflicts with nuclear weapons. Royal Little became acquainted with Gavin while the general was head of Research and Development in the Pentagon when Little's Textron was a major supplier to the military. Little got him interested in ADL and, in 1958, Gavin became a vice-president of ADL and a member of its board.

Less than one year later, Gavin became the Company's first executive vice president, and by early 1960, its president. However, he was in that position only a short time because the newly elected president, John Kennedy, asked him to take the post of Ambassador to France. Gavin was given an eighteen-month leave of absence from ADL but was permitted to keep his seat on the board.

When General Gavin returned in 1962, he became CEO. Some say he was not about to change the Company, but was primarily looking out for the interests of Royal Little. Gavin often held meetings with key personnel to discuss matters in which Little might have an interest. While his basic idea was to avoid unnecessary surprise to Little and reduce the likelihood of ill-informed or adverse reactions, he also started to think about turning ADL into a large international company.

General Gavin was the first to push the idea of combining the talents of the technology and business consulting areas of the Company to create a strong competitive advantage. At the same time, he recognized that these were two entirely different cul- tures with a huge gap between them. He understood that the greatest obstacle to progress at ADL was the cadre of section heads who wanted to protect their domains.

While Gavin did not make significant internal changes within ADL, he made up for this through his image and his connections to the outside. Gavin had a remarkable ability to communicate with all walks of life and did so with great charm and persuasion. He was a likable fellow who showed interest in the professional work that was being done and was willing to help others. His door was always open to staff members for advice, although many discussions ended with one of the general's war stories.

One example of the impact of Gavin's reputation was seen in 1968 when ADL was working on a major proposal to Saudi Arabia. Harland Riker, the local manager, felt that the chances would be enhanced if General Gavin could visit with some of the Saudi officials. Gavin, however, observed that he preferred to deal at the top and would only visit with King Faisal. This was easier said than done since Riker could not get past the king's chief or protocol. By coincidence, a Massachusetts citizens group had proposed General Gavin as a presidential candidate, and the news had made it to the cover of *Business Week* magazine. When a copy of the magazine arrived in Riyadh, Riker rushed it to the chief of protocol and convinced him that it was in his best interests to arrange a meeting between the king and the future President of the United States. The ploy was successful.

The general was also a great success at cocktail parties, although not always with the desired results. At one Washington occasion, some celebrities were invited to meet the general—including Ken Galbraith and Arthur Schlesinger who were both well-known ladies' men. However, ten minutes into the reception, all the men seemed to be talking among themselves. The lady guests, on the other hand, were clustered, open-eyed, around magnetic Jim Gavin.

Despite his deep interest in research and technology, General Gavin was never really at home in ADL's environment. Although the

Company was doing very well—growing rapidly and expanding internationally, many felt that major changes were necessary to carry on the legacy of being the oldest consulting firm in the world. Nobody had the answer and while Gavin pondered the broad aspects of the business, politically oriented staff members poised themselves for an opportunity to jump to the top post.

John Magee

At a Washington cocktail party where John Magee was the principal guest, it soon became apparent to the host that John was not at ease among all the small talk. As a gracious host, he wondered how to make his guest more comfortable. By chance, his 15 year-old stepson appeared on the scene and whispered that he was in great need of help with his math homework: "Can you take a few minutes away from your guest?" The host had a better solution. "I have a math expert who can help you." For the next twenty minutes, there was John Magee, ADL President, now happy in his own mètier, helping a teenager with differential calculus.

John Magee was a Ph.D. in mathematical statistics who had worked as a financial analyst at the Johns-Manville building products division before joining ADL in 1950. Soon after that he co-authored an article with Cyril Herrmann of MIT for the *Harvard Business Review*. Dealing with the applications of operations research to management, the article opened a door for him in ADL's emerging operations research practice. Once Magee came into the OR group, it grew to 350 staff members with a focus on solving management problems. At the same time, the technical and scientific professionals did not appreciate this new growth trend in the Company.

John Magee had a brilliant mind but many felt that he was not a politician. Some of his colleagues described him as a self-centered "Brahmin" intellectual who preferred not to get into dirty work. Others noted that he was a pure rationalist and needed to see a completely logical flow of thought. One staff member who presented proposals to him felt as if he was being tested every time.

Magee is said to have had a good understanding of the corporate system and to have used it to get rid of the people who stood in the way of his career goals. One story is that he maneuvered the head of the Operations Research section into a foreign assignment and, during his absence, took his place. When the colleague returned, he found himself left out.

Whether he was a politician or not, Magee is said to have worked hard to take the position of president from Howard McMahon who was viewed as a scientist and not as a manager. Some say that when McMahon felt cornered he often made unfortunate decisions that made him look even worse, and that Magee took advantage of this situation. Once installed as President, Magee coveted the position of CEO, at the time held by Gavin. Again, he did not spare energy to go after it.

By 1972, with the retirement of General Gavin approaching, Royal Little had become concerned with the managerial future of the Company, but he did not feel that Magee would make a good CEO. Little wanted to bring in somebody from the outside. Together with

Gavin, Little identified ADL Board member Eli Goldston, the widely respected and talented CEO of Eastern Gas & Fuel Associates, as their chosen candidate to run ADL. Goldston held Harvard degrees in economics, law, and business management. Since the ADL staff largely shared Little's negative view of Magee, there was much excitement about Goldston's selection. It was felt that he would provide much needed direction to the future evolvement of the Company. Then, shortly before starting the job, Goldston died. This event, opening the door for Magee to become CEO, was seen by many as a great setback for the Company.[1]

With the exception of General Gavin, John Magee was the first CEO at ADL without an engineering degree. For this reason, one would expect him to be able to move the Company away from the process thinking that had dominated the Company throughout its existence. As an operations researcher, Magee would be able to focus on end results and markets rather than processes. However, ADL's efforts to move away from process thinking were not particularly successful. Having been shaped by a decade of moving up through the Company ranks, Magee did not have the business acumen characteristic of corporate executives with wider management experience. Although he tried to bring ADL up to date in the marketplace, this effort was not successful. As one of his colleagues later noted, he earned the dubious distinction of presiding over 11 years of declining margins.

Magee had a reputation for being a good listener who could change his mind if good arguments were presented. He seemed to feel good in small groups and one-on-one conversations, but appeared remote to large groups. At one time, he moved his office from the executive wing to another building so as to be closer to the people. At lunch, he often joined groups in the cafeteria and participated in their discussions. He was very analytical and tough and would do what he considered was right despite opposition. When one section head complained to Magee about ADL moving outside consulting areas—such as ADL Systems—he was relieved from his management position and left the Company soon thereafter.

---

[1] When Magee became CEO, Gavin was relegated to spend the years remaining until his retirement in offices that some considered unsuitable for his stature.

Instead of focusing on something that ADL excelled in, for example, operations research, Magee spearheaded the overall expansion in the early '80s—especially in the newly emerging biotechnology and life sciences fields. Magee thought that the field of biotechnology, along with health care, would be huge, like the later information technology boom. This expansion to a new area required investment in expensive laboratories and had an adverse effect on the bottom line.

For example, to make ADL a serious contender in the area of health care services, Magee acquired the Lester Gorsline Company of California in 1969. It was thought that its systems support capabilities would be a profitable line of business. However, Gorsline's business depended on government subsidies to health service organizations. Soon after ADL bought it, these subsidies stopped, as did Gorsline's profitability.

Another acquisition that ran out of steam was Stoller Associates, a small nuclear power consulting firm. As the nation's embrace of nuclear technology waned, it became a cash drain. ADL sold it back to its employees in 1983 at $900,000 below its book value.

Another problem was Magee's interest in having the Company go public. The public offering raised money for the Company at a time when it was not needed. ADL could have used the money for expansion, such as by acquiring new activities, but the money was never used for this purpose. At the same time, going public made its poor performance some years later known to the competitors who took advantage of it.

One of the means by which Magee tried to change to Company was by expanding the role of subsidiaries. Since its early days, ADL had formed subsidiaries, but they were seldom successful. For example, Dr. Little formed the American Viscose Company and the Cellulose Products Company. The idea to capitalize on ADL's technical developments was a good one, but most of the ventures that ADL started up failed when they ran out of money.[2]

---

[2] In the '20s, ADL took equity positions in some ventures it had helped to set up for clients. For the most part, however, ADL's business had been selling professional services.

When Magee became the CEO, he put Charlie Kensler in charge of professional services and concentrated almost entirely on acquiring or setting up subsidiaries. With the exception of one or two, they were not successful. The reason was that ADL was in the business of selling professional services, and good consultants, especially technical ones, do not necessarily make good operating managers. Conventional wisdom would have it that consultants who are good at advising others could also do so for themselves. However, this proved not to be the case. ADL's failure to apply its expertise to its own management would turn out to be one more reason for its eventual downfall.

Kensler became the legendary cigar-smoking VP who seemed to personally know what projects everybody was working on and who kept a status report on everybody and everything in his head. Kensler pushed for billability within sections and prowled the halls, dropping into people's offices in a seemingly unplanned way. He also he kept himself informed by shuttling among the lunch tables in ADL's cafeteria, the place where many projects were created or planned and where people sometimes found their next assignment.

Kensler was seen as being tough, but also fair and easy to deal with. He could sort things out very quickly and was quick to act if he found that somebody was misleading him. Magee relied on him to do the dirty work, and some blame Kensler for the fact that a few valuable professionals who could not work with him left the Company.

The Magee-Kensler combination did not make enough investment in the Company in terms of restructuring and cost cutting. Furthermore, the two did not always work together as a team, and at some instances did not talk to each other for weeks at a time.

Another failure was Magee's attempt to diversify into the rapidly growing computer systems area. He formed a subsidiary, ADL Systems, to develop information systems related to the processing of health care claims and other information technology. While the idea was to establish a business unit that was not dependent on the vagaries of professional service income, it was not able to hold its own in a competitive market and was dissolved a few years later.

The ADL Board criticized John Magee for the ADL Systems debacle and, as a result, he rejected suggestions to fund similar activities. This reluctance probably contributed to the fact that ADL's Information Technology practice did not keep pace with the growing and lucrative activities of its competitors. While other consulting firms expanded their information technology practices by acquiring smaller companies, ADL's work in that practice area was slowly phased out.

In 1978, ADL acquired the official Company limousine, a grey Checker cab with a reading lamp mounted over the rear seat— selected personally by John Magee who used it frequently.

Magee's view of ADL's management values was reflected in a speech he made in 1981. He emphasized research, information, management of intellectual properties, and helping people in adversary or negotiating situations. He said that the only thing he could be certain about was that it was essentially impossible to set bounds on the work that ADL would do. While this sounded great to the scientists who enjoyed the variety of projects that came in the door, it was ominous for others who wanted to see some focused direction to help ADL strengthen its position in a climate of growing competition.

Magee provided no real leadership and was satisfied with maintaining the status quo. This was reflected in the lack of dynamics in the company itself. Unlike some of the earlier Company leaders who initiated new developments, such as in flavor and helium, the Company under Magee stressed the cultivation of a few established clients and did not seek out new areas of business. When brought under pressure, Magee was likely to become defensive and fall back on his position of authority. In one such situation, he is reported to have said, "Even if I agreed with that point, I would ignore it. I am the President."

The ADL managers in Europe generally felt that Magee never seriously tried to manage the Company. As one result, they saw no development of a significant management consulting capability, which would have greatly reinforced similar European initiatives. ADL Europe had become a major competitor to McKinsey, Boston Consulting Group and others in Europe and the fact that ADL U.S. never remotely reached that status was a handicap to their world-wide efforts. European managers were left to define and implement their own future directions. They did not mind doing that, but they felt that Cambridge, under Magee, was more of a hindrance than a support.[3]

Charles LaMantia

Charlie was pretty good at making jokes, but his words of wisdom often fell flat. In an interview in the Metalworking Magazine in August, 1996, he formulated his view of effective management as follows: "The key to competitiveness in the global game is not downsizing, but accelerating continuous performance improvement through employee input, and through that input, growth."

When the ADL Board looked for a replacement for Magee, they wanted a candidate who knew the Company. Lou Rambo, the personnel director, was placed in charge of finding the replacement, and some consider this a major mistake. Rambo may have figured that the candidate had to be somebody who would not overshadow Magee.[4] The Board eventually approved LaMantia who had left ADL four years earlier for the CEO position of the process systems subsidiary of Koch, his former client.[5] As one senior staff member commented, "Charlie was good at tennis, but not at running a company. He was suspicious, stiff, insecure and arrogant."

Having been appointed president in 1986, LaMantia wanted to demonstrate a financial turnaround and started by cutting the

---

[3] Especially in the eighties, the quality of work coming out of Cambridge and carried out in the European markets was very uneven at best. European managers often feared the involvement of U.S. colleagues. Magee was aware of the quality problems, but was not effective in taking corrective action.

[4] The top candidates included Dick Heitman who declined because he was not interested in administrative work, Al Wechsler who was being endorsed by Charlie Kensler, and Charlie LaMantia.

[5] Koch started the subsidiary in part on the basis of a cryogenics technology developed at ADL.

staff. "He cut the biochemistry, as well as economic development and any other activity he did not understand," one staff member recalls." He focused on plumbing."

LaMantia presented himself as a consensus builder and, in the initial interview after becoming president, he stated that he would emphasize "empowerment and delegation of responsibility and authority as far down into the organization as possible." This raised the eyebrows of traditional managers who had been taught that responsibility could not be delegated.

Although LaMantia's door was always open and he was easy to talk to, it seemed that he was never listening. While he was always polite and grateful for comments brought to him, he never appeared to act on them. On several occasions, he is said to have interfered with lower level decisions without consulting the affected executives.

Some people who were close to LaMantia felt that he did a superb job by tightening management across-the-board, reducing central overhead and introducing a rational incentive system. While this success is still appreciated by ADLers, it is generally accepted that he failed when he tried to change the focus of the Company to become a big business. As one staff member commented, "Charlie wanted to change the ADL culture following the McKinsey example. He could have started a new activity, but he wanted to change the 'old' ADLers."

Others feel that LaMantia got a good start, but that he should have stepped down after four to five years. Faced with declining business and unable to change the Company, he kept shuffling the organization and concentrating on the control of operations. Educated as a chemical engineer, LaMantia looked at ADL's entire operation as processes and designed elaborate organizational schemes including divisions, groups, directorates, and various committees, as well as complicated financial incentives intended to work as control mechanisms. Responding to the changing markets was not his priority.

Process thinking

The management style that characterized the early years of ADL as well as the final years under Charlie LaMantia, can be best characterized as "process thinking". From a management viewpoint, it could not stand up in a competitive environment.

Many of those who have worked with people educated as engineers and others with degrees in business, have probably noted that there are marked differences how the two personality types approach problems and resolve issues. In the many years that I have worked with engineers, I have appreciated their attention to details that eventually build up to a working whole. At the same time, I have been frustrated by the engineers' desire to over-engineer beyond the requirements of the customer and to tweak the design after it has been completed. Sometimes, especially from a business viewpoint, the process becomes more important than the end result.

Unlike the engineers, managers are concerned with the market and the ability to provide a service or product at a cost that will produce a satisfactory profit. While the manager will pay attention to the process of producing that profit, he has to juggle many balls and the process is only the means to an end. Engineers, who have been trained in a discipline such as chemical processing, are particularly prone to look at management as a process. To them, if the organizational processes are properly designed and controlled, everything should fall into place for a profitable operation. This kind of process-oriented thinking may be constrained to a single thread. Introducing them to dynamic alternatives, as often happens in management situations, may confuse their detailed assessment of the situation and result in less than optimum outcome.

This kind of limitation was illustrated by a chemical process engineer with whom I had traveled to Canada. The weather had been bad and, as we tried to reconnect at Chicago's O'Hare Airport, we were faced with delays and cancellations. As the situation kept changing, I tried to make the best of it by rushing from one airline to another, making and changing reservations, so as to be able to continue as soon as possible. My engineering colleague, who had been trailing me, suddenly stopped and looked at me in bewilderment. "Can you tell me what is going on? I can only take one thing at a time."

The situation was simple and direct during the first fifty years when the Company was in a growth market and its reputation helped it to hold its own against new competitors. By 1970, however, the competition had intensified and the consulting industry had become more dynamic. An important growth area in this period was information technology and systems, and those consulting firms that did not have this capability looked for ways to acquire it. This meant that many smaller companies were bought up, significantly changing the slate of services offered by traditional consultants. Being successful in this environment required thinking that was not constrained by traditional processes.

Process thinking involves identification, categorization, and prioritization of business functions, linking them through their informational needs and setting up control points. This is very much like designing the vessels, connecting piping and the control valves in a chemical processing plant. Management thinking, on the other hand, makes use of, creates, modifies and tailors the functionalities to achieve a given goal.

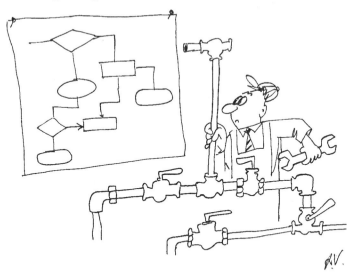

LaMantia's organizational designs were not simple. In one instance, he offered "integrating strategies that included a unified company image, cross selling and integration of the business units, making them into separate sister concerns, developing a cross-business synergy, product, and practice, and a single company strategy—a global industry practice." The underlying idea was that ADL's strength lay in its vast and varied knowledge, which could be utilized across the different business units. It just did not come off that way.

These process designs were expected to allow the company to focus on its client relationships, bring in business, and generate profits in the areas where ADL had already shown success. Unlike a chemical plant, however, where the processes can be mathematically calculated, the consulting business depends on human resources and interactions that are much less predictable. As the marketplace changed, ADL was not able to keep up with it.

Things went differently in Europe where the ADL management had formed its own executive board and did not want their operations constrained by the processes used in Cambridge. In the mid-nineties, when the ADL's US management consulting practice was losing money and LaMantia was trying to fine-tune it through a series of re-organizations, the European management consulting practice grew by leaps and bounds.[6]

LaMantia was suspicious of the ADL Alumni Association that had been formed a few years before he became the CEO and he did not know how to deal with it. The officers of the association met with him each year to discuss ways of cooperation that would benefit each organization. The meetings were courteous but somewhat strained and did not lead to any results.

After a few years, when it was obvious that the alumni association was not in competition with ADL, some cooperation developed. ADL published an official alumni directory, issued a special alumni edition of the *Little Paper*, and appointed an alumni coordinator. Some other avenues for cooperation with the alumni were suggested, but were not actively pursued.

---

[6] Ironically, the most successful leader of the European operations, Tom Sommerlatte, had an undergraduate degree in chemical engineering, as well as an MBA. However, he was never constrained by process thinking and, at one point, even tried to raise funds to enable ADL to participate in the operation of East German factories. Such a diversion from traditional management consulting would have never been permitted in Cambridge.

In 1990, ADL held an elaborate alumni party but did not involve the alumni association in the planning and did not even acknowledge its existence. The party was plush, held in the ballroom of the Ritz Carlton and attended by hundreds. In his usual withdrawn manner, LaMantia did not behave as a gracious host, but hung out in the back with some of his vice presidents. Ivars Avots, the alumni association president, used this opportunity to circulate near the entrance and greet the guests. At the end of the event, many came up to him to thank the alumni association for a great party.

CHAPTER 8

Shuffling the Boxes

"...this is a relatively simple business among the spectrum of businesses we could pursue. So let's not make it any more complicated than it has to be."[1]

When Little & Walker started their company, they had a staff of only seven employees. To make the organization look more impressive, they set them up in seven separate departments.[2] As the Company grew and new employees were added to the staff, Little added a new roster of departments.[3]

This increasing complexity of the organization was helped by the fact that Royal Little, the nephew of Dr. Little, had become active in the Company. His success in building up the Textron Corporation led *The Wall Street Journal* to call him the inventor of the modern conglomerate. While ADL was nowhere near being a conglomerate, Royal Little was shaping its image so that ADL could take a place among the industrial leaders.

Building an image is one thing, but running a consulting firm is quite another. By 1936, the image was built up sufficiently to go after the big game. ADL was reorganized, its stock put into a trust, and its operating structure changed to better deal with the tasks on

---

[1] CEO Charles LaMantia in a February 6, 1989, presentation on the state of the firm.
[2] Analytical, Coal and Derivatives, Lubrication, Biology, Textiles, Engineering, and Papermaking.
[3] Textile, Fuel Engineering, Gas Engineering, General Laboratory, Research, and Paper and Pulp.

hand. Previously, everybody had reported directly to Dr. Little. Now, sections were set up according to scientific disciplines, reporting to Earl Stevenson. The analytical work that had formed the main activity for the previous fifty years was turned over to an outside group of former employees. From now on, emphasis was to be placed on contract research arrangements for big corporations like Owens-Illinois.

The strategy worked and the Company continued to grow. In the mid-fifties, Stevenson brought in a consultant to study ADL's internal organization. He was particularly interested in whether ADL should shift emphasis from technological research to management consulting. The consultant found that about a third of ADL's work already consisted of management consulting. This finding turned management attention to business areas other than research and development and can be viewed as a critical point in the evolution of ADL.

Stevenson had a vision of the Company diversifying beyond what Dr. Little had set up and wanted ADL to become a postwar engine of growth for US industry through technology. The major part of ADL's management consulting at the time was Operations Research. It had been introduced by Ray Stevens who was impressed by the success of OR during the war and felt it would also help to solve peacetime problems. The OR group was started with the understanding that, even if it operated at a loss, management would support it for three years.

The OR group got its real boost through work ADL had done for Sears Roebuck. The retailer was about to invest a million dollars in a new method for producing antifreeze but ADL discovered that it was a sham. Pleased with the report, Sears Roebuck asked ADL to improve its catalogue distribution system that presented a classic OR problem. As a result, Sears Roebuck was a major customer for the group until the seventies when the catalogue business was discontinued.

In 1958, when General Gavin came aboard as a vice-president and a member of the board, his eyes were mostly on research and development, his major interests while in the army. However, he soon came to realize that ADL was turning into a management consulting organization. By 1960, when he became ADL's president, research and development assignments were being outpaced by management consulting. During the organizational shuffling that took place during this time, John Magee garnered the leadership of the Operations Research section, opening the door to management consulting activities even further.

The ADL organization grew reflecting the increasing variety of its activities. By 1960, it had six divisions with a vice-president in charge of each. They were Research and Development, Engineering, Life Sciences, Energy and Materials, Advanced Research, and Management Services. Despite the titles, the Company still looked like a technology rather than a management consulting firm. This did not change until ten years later when the technical divisions were reduced to three: Engineering, Life Sciences, and Research and Development. At the same time, management consulting had expanded to three divisions: Management Services, Management Counseling, and Industrial and Regional Economics. An International Division had also been added. While this was a bold step for the Company, one could not ignore the fact that other consulting firms had grown much faster and had moved past ADL.

Within the divisions, ADL still remained largely unstructured. Howard McMahon, who became president in 1965, had set up a collegial business model and pushed quality whereby individuals and groups developed their own niches. It was a common saying that there were 600 highly individual professionals sharing an office building with the section managers trying to impose some sort of accountability.

A new activity, the Management Education Institute (MEI) was formed in 1961 to train foreign nationals under the auspices of the U.S. Agency for International Development. The initial idea was to have some American university or college run the program, but the number of students grew and the collaboration did not work out. By 1973, MEI had become an institution in its own right and was the only private, profit-making organization in Massachusetts accredited to grant the degree of master of science in management.

The Seventies

The Company became more structured in the '70s. The section heads were still running the day-to-day operations, but they often had unit managers reporting to them, as well as a layer of directors and practice managers gradually built up above them. This departmentalization had an effect on casework. To increase billability, management sometimes loaded cases with people that were not selected by the case leaders. Getting authorization to use experts from outside the Company to participate in casework became more difficult.

The lead management committee that looked at all incoming business became all-powerful. Unless there was a serious challenge, once the committee assigned the lead to a particular section, it pretty much stayed there. In the '60s, case leaders had looked for the most capable participants for their cases not only from their own sections but from other parts of the company as well. With the greater structure came accounting procedures and performance incentives that favored keeping all the work within a section. Thus, some cases were loaded up with people who were not ideally qualified to do the work, but just happened to be available.

The size of the consulting market during the '70s had increased from $2 billion to $40 billion, and there were many new entrants. Unlike ADL, these consulting companies focused on specific segments of management consulting and specialized in a few particular areas. The new entrants also had the effect of segmenting the market into core functional components. Since ADL was a broad-based, non-specific product company, it was able to capture many business problems that arose as markets evolved. For the time being, ADL felt his gave them a distinct advantage in the market. Fundamentally, however, ADL was dependent on its past reputation, the vast knowledge base represented by its staff, and a good R&D facility.

The Choir of Angels

In 1972, Charlie Kensler, who had been appointed Chief Professional Officer, decided that the divisions were spending too much effort competing among themselves. Kensler also felt that the division heads were wasting time since they were neither managing nor performing client work. He abolished the divisions and substituted them with more or less autonomus operating sections. They included such new practice areas as Health Care, Energy, and Environment.

Kensler assigned the division heads and a few other senior staff members to a newly established Corporate Staff. He centralized control by having all the sections report directly to him. Previously, the division heads had met regularly as the Corporate Management Team, but now they were no longer part of management. They did not have any specifically assigned functions other than to mentor the sections from which they came and look for new clients. Since they were accountable for their own billability, they worked on cases just like other staff members. They soon called themselves the "Choir of Angels."

ADL management missed the point that when the divisions were abolished and operations were centralized, ADL's feudal power structure was lost. A strong management team was needed to bring everybody together and thrive under the new conditions. Such a team never materialized.

Another unique change in the seventies was the establishment of the Program Systems Management Company (PSMC) This was the brainchild of Albert Kelley, a former Navy pilot, NASA project manager and dean of the School of Business at Boston College. His idea was to start large-scale programs and projects for the military and other government agencies, as well as the large construction companies. Having been burned by a series of unsuccessful subsidiaries, John Magee thought that PSMC could provide the entry to a new and profitable business in governmental programs and projects. Unfortunately, Kelley's view of the outside world was limited by his specific experience, and he did not know much about hands-on project management. Ignoring the fact that this had a negative effect on the project management consulting activities already in progress, his idea was to go after supposedly lucrative multi-million dollar projects.

The new group was favored with a reduced overhead rate and performance targets. It was staffed largely with retired military officers and people that happened to be politically expedient. For example, a newly hired relative of a leading Massachusetts official did not spend much time in the office and his responsibilities were never disclosed. PSMC also never really fit into the ADL framework and was viewed as a second-class citizen by the rest of the staff.

A few contracts with the military kept PSMC going until 1988 when it experienced a big boost in income. Eventually, the group was reorganized into the Public Programs Management Company that worked on large multi-year contracts from the U.S. Post Office, IRS and the South Carolina Research Authority. Kelley was made a senior vice president before leaving ADL to take an appointed position at the Defense Department.

The eighties

The demand for consulting services continued to grow, and the ADL organization grew with it. By 1980, there were thirty oper- ating sections including many new areas of activity. There was also a growing number of vice presidents. It was said that once a vice president, always a vice president, unless you quit the Company.

Sadly for the people involved, the title did not carry with it all the perks awarded by other companies.[4]

As the consulting market expanded, ADL lost its dominant position and continued to slide. New companies tooled with contemporary technologies, skills, identifiable products, and a singular image gained market strength. ADL's pride derived from the freshness of its approach to each case, the "Eureka" kind of solution, and not undertaking repetitive jobs. Nevertheless, follow-on work and additional work for previous clients accounted for the greatest part of ADL's business.

In 1980, Kensler was starting to plan for his retirement and began to look for a replacement. Charlie LaMantia and Al Wechsler were his best candidates. When Wechsler was appointed senior vice president, LaMantia was left out and resigned to take a position with one of his clients. Wechsler's new job was ambiguous and difficult. For the next five years, he gradually took over the function of the Chief Professional Officer, but Kensler made sure he was not left out of any major decisions. After Wechsler's appointment, the Corporate Staff was dissolved and its members moved back into the sections.

When LaMantia became president, he followed the practice established in the European operations and set up three major directorates: North American Management Consulting, Technology and Product Development, and Environmental Consulting. Since he gave them power to compete with each other, they set up their own personnel staffs and became fief- doms duplicating some of the functions carried out at the corporate level. Separate sales teams were set up, and the well-established case leader functions were split up between client relations and case management. While this was accompanied by a rational incentive system, the rigid structure ran against the ADL tradition and required players that represented a different organizational culture. In particular, it

---

[4] In 1958, Cy Herrman was made a vice president. He had been a section manager at the time and to avoid the possibility that other section managers would also expect titles, he had to give up management of the section. In later years, all section heads were given the title of vice president, and the title was also given to selected professionals who did not have any management responsibilities.

widened the gap between the traditional research and development sections and the management consultants who often viewed their technical colleagues as second-class citizens. Some believe that ADL's later difficulties can be traced to LaMantia's decision to emulate McKinsey and other consulting companies and put science and technology on the back burner.

In comparison to the European operations, the Cambridge staff did not show the same level of motivation and cameraderie. LaMantia had already adopted the European directorate structure, and now he formally added the concept of professional practices. Practice leaders were responsible for staff training and quality of work, but not for profitability.

When the various actions did not produce the desired results, Charlie LaMantia again shuffled the organization. This time, his objective was to create an organizational structure that had more accountability, identified specific goals and duties, and improved resource allocation. To accomplish this, he introduced a vague concept described as vertical development and functional orientation. Seven directorates were grouped into three major businesses. Five of the directorates were related to management consulting and were geographically structured. The entire Company structure was tied together with seven common business processes, such as developing staff, managing client work, managing finances, etc. Senior vice presidents were assigned to oversee the processes. Additional management initiatives included overhauling the financial area, as well as improving planning, budgeting, and accounting.

A new career structure was announced to bring together specific functions, responsibilities and performance expect-ations. The professional ranks now included three positions: consultant, senior consultant, and director.[5] Line management positions, such as vice president and section head, were said to offer further growth opportunities. This time, the new titles came with incentive compensation that could boost income for a job well done. Potential career

---

[5] In Europe where the director concept had started, the existing directors elected directors from a pool of candidates who usually had proven themselves in the position of associate director. In Cambridge, management appointed the directors and the associate director position was not established until later.

paths were spelled out for the first time in Cambridge and professional training courses were set up to support personnel development. However, in a culture of independent thinkers, the concept never caught on to the extent it had in Europe and, once again, did not bring the expected results.

In the new organizational lineup, all professional services directorates reported directly to CEO Charlie LaMantia. Each client case would primarily belong to one directorate but would encompass different business processes, making it a matrix-type structure. While most of the rest of the organizational structure and players with executive responsibility remained unchanged, this could not be said of the operational processes. To provide a mechanism for focusing market development and networking activities across and between the directorates, LaMantia introduced the concept of practice areas. A Marketing Council was set up to work with the Marketing and Corporate Communications Department to improve the Company's image and make the image consonant with ADL's strategic focus. The Council was also charged with developing a market planning process for use by the practices, sections, and offices.

LaMantia also thought that ADL needed to develop and apply modern quality control techniques to its consulting work and administration. He formed a Corporate Quality Council, headed by Al Wechsler, that would set goals and recommend approaches for the conduct of consulting work, analyze the causes of overruns, and establish a corporate improvement program for all client work and internal activities.

After some more thought, he set up a Staff Development Task Force chaired by Harland Riker to develop generic and functional consulting skills training programs.[6] Next, he set up the Profit and Loss Leadership Task group, chaired by Scott Stricoff. It was to promote profits by organizing biweekly and annual managers meetings. Last but not least, a Compensation Committee, chaired by Ashok Kalelkar, was set up to work on a contingent compensation program

---

[6] A career stage structure and related professional development programs had been successfully used in Europe. This approach had been successful in motivating the staff and creating a sense of camaraderie and had been given credit for the rapid growth of the European operations.

that would be tied to career levels, but also take into consideration variable compensation based on corporate and directorate performance. Payments to each directorate's staff would be based on the individual's relative performance within the directorate.

Instead of aiming at specific goals, a lot of effort was spent on improving the processes. The needs of new markets and responses to competitive pressures were not given appropriate attention. Also, one could only wonder if such capable consultants as Wechsler, Kalelkar and Stricoff had any time left to devote to the substance that the name of ADL carried to the world.

The nineties

ADL went into 1991 after a glowing year. The Company had 36 offices and project locations worldwide, with a staff of 2540. Total revenues had increased 13% to $358 million, while income had risen 50%. Little notice was being given to the fact that most of the staff expansion and nearly half of the business had taken place outside the United States. The Company was still being run with a focus on Cambridge. It elected 12 new corporate vice presidents and hired a Director of Marketing who had previously served at the Bank of Boston.

In the United States, the fastest growing practice area in this period was environmental consulting. By the end of 1990, this area had over 100 staff members and more were being sought for Canada and Europe. ADL conducted seminars and training courses that were attended by more than 2500 professionals from over 100 companies. The Training Institute for Environmental, Health and Safety Management was set up with the aim of getting even greater visibility for the courses being offered. Nothing indicated that the environmental market would collapse a few years later.

The directorate that eventually had the greatest effect on the profitability of ADL's US operations was North American Management Consulting. During the eighties, ADL had employed a "harvest" strategy that had cut down on investment in the development of clients, staff and intellectual capital. At the same time, management made efforts to go after large and structured cases that clashed with the ADL culture. As the performance results deteriorated, the leadership of the practice area was changed frequently: Elliott Wilbur, Ashok Kalelkar, Tammy Erickson, Bruce Grant and finally David Robinson. Some of them tried to improve the financial picture by cutting costs and eliminating many of the marketing, staff and service development programs that had been built up over the years. At the same time, Charlie LaMantia had made financial commitments to the ADL Board that left little room for investment in the '90s.

"We were balancing on a tightrope," recalls Tammy Erickson. "We tried to make as much investment as we possibly could afford, but had to balance that against aggressive performance targets. If we slipped even a little bit in terms of performance, there was no safety net."

At the end of 1993, LaMantia came out with another major reorganization. The Corporate Management Group and the Corporate Operating group were replaced by a Senior Leadership and Management Team. It had ten members who were responsible for the formulation and implementation of strategy and policy for operations and business processes. In addition, they met as the Human Resources Policy Committee and the Marketing and Product Development Committee.

To top it all off, an Office of the President was formed to provide oversight for the directorates and subsidiaries. Looking at the responsibilities the members of this group were assigned, it seemed that each was given the responsibility for those areas with which they were least familiar. Charlie LaMantia took over the oversight of European and the ADL Enterprises activities. Al Wechsler, an engineer, looked after Asia-Pacific operations and the Management Education Institute. Only Ashok Kalelkar continued with the technology and product areas that he was well familiar with, but he also was charged to look after North American Management Consulting and Latin American consulting.

Between 1985 and 1992, ADL's earnings growth had been 15% a year and the stock had gone up to nearly $150. However, sales growth did not keep up with earnings growth, and earnings growth could not be sustained until sales growth matched it. At a management meeting, the decision was reached to change the focus from the $30–50,000 cases to those that could steadily bring in $1–3 million a year. Sales teams of two to three people were set up to work with such potential clients emulating the activity of the big competitors. This did not work out because ADL did not have the same kind of people that were successful in other companies. Much money was invested, but sales actually declined. The incentive program and MDT exasperated the problem and induced good people to leave the Company. It also caused infighting between groups vying for business.

By now, ADL had fallen far back behind other companies in the thriving corporate strategy business, but that did not stop it from inventing new approaches. In 1994, LaMantia adopted the "One Strategy" program to integrate strategy, products, and training across the Company's management consulting business worldwide. He also formed the "SLAM—Senior Leadership and Management Team" that included the heads of the directorates and a few top executives and charged them with an oversight responsibility over the directorates.

In 1995, ADL responded to the flashy ads by Andersen Consulting and others by setting up a corporate marketing function and initiating aggressive moves towards establishing a better image.[7] Two years earlier, ADL had brought in Alan Friedman, formerly of Wang Laboratories, to replace Lew Rambo as vice president and director of human resources. Although Friedman's view of the world was much more money oriented than LaMantia's, he became the closest confidant and advisor to the chief executive.

Another outsider, Allen Steinmetz, was brought in to spike up ADL marketing and build a new image for the Company. The key to his campaign was the "pathway to performance" theme. New brochures and stories were developed around the pathway theme, but since the newcomers did not understand the culture of the Company,

---

[7] Among other actions, ADL promoted a book *Unwritten Rules of the Game*. Written by staffer Peter Scott-Morgan, the book maintained that corporate change programs often fail because executives ignore the powerful unwritten rules that govern their organizations. In retrospect, one may wish that the ADL executives had read it.

they made mistakes and met resistance from staff members. For example, an editor was sent to Moscow to develop a brochure for the Russian market. Working together with a local photographer, he came up with a very pretty publication. Local ADL staff members, however, felt that the brochure did not apply to the work that was being done and was, in fact, insulting to some of the potential clients. Meantime, back in Cambridge, all offices were plastered with pictures of a path winding through orchards and forests. Copies were passed out to the clients. Little figures of a roadrunner on the pathway were handed out to executives. In all, "the pathway" cost around $6 million and was a dismal failure.

In 1996, LaMantia made another attempt to differentiate the firm from others in the market through an initiative called One-Company Management Platform. The idea was to integrate the firm's management consulting work with its organizational change and learning expertise and the company's leadership position in technology and innovation. This would be accomplished by imposing on top of its existing organizational structure a matrix consisting of four strategic thrusts: key-client management, global and regional industry practices, global functional practices, and regional market management.

All this monkey business did not make up for the fact that, since the seventies, ADL did not have a clear strategy for growth. For example, the technically oriented top management missed the opportunity to move into the lucrative business of strategy consulting. Others, such as Boston Consulting Group, moved into this practice area ahead of ADL and became very successful.[8] The images of the American and European parts of ADL diverged more and more. In America, the outside world still looked at ADL as technology gurus while in Europe the focus was on management consulting.

The success of ADL in Europe would not have happened without Tom Sommerlatte. A chemical engineer with an MBA degree, he had grown up in France, Belgium and the United States and, in 1973, was one of the founders of the ADL office in Germany. During his

---

[8] Bruce Henderson who started Boston Consulting Group came from ADL.

leadership the sales and profits rose 20–25% each year. He noted at the time that a company whose business was more than 65% outside the United States could no longer be guided by the principles from New England. This did not sit well with Cambridge.

In mid-nineties, a conflict developed between Tom Sommerlatte and Charlie Kensler who felt that, despite growing revenues, the European operations were not generating enough profit. Kensler did not recognize the European business culture, often based on tax considerations, that encouraged executive perks, elaborate training programs, and expensive off-site meetings. As a result of the conflict, Sommerlatte lost his European top management position and in 1966 was named the executive chairman of the Global Management Consulting practice.

Aside from the fact that profits from the European operations were often financing Cambridge, the Europeans also had another axe to grind. Although ADL withdrew its stock from the public in 1988, it continued to operate like a public corporation. The European partners owned a share of the Company but they could not participate in the management decisions.[9] In many respects, they were in a worse position than minority stockholders who at least could bring up their voices at the annual meeting. If anybody did that that at ADL, they could be expected to be shown out the door.

This situation was brought home to Tom Sommerlatte who, only a year after becoming the executive chairman of the consulting business, had an argument with Charlie LaMantia. The new CEO said he wanted to bring the company "back to its roots" by combining the practices of technology, environment and management consulting. Tom Sommerlatte disagreed with this approach, and as a result, was relieved of his executive position. Dietmar Fink, a professor at the Management Consulting Institute in Bonn, noted that ADL which was so proud of its multicultural teams had become a prime example of dysfunctional international cooperation.

The professor also observed that the reason that ADL had functioned so well, despite its autocratic management style, was that

---

[9] MDT owned the controlling shares of the Company, but regulations did not permit foreigners to be members of MDT.

there was very little hierarchial culture in the dispersed areas of the Company. He noted that ADL had excellent staff, a fine reputation, and good connections to its clients. To bring such a firm down, he noted, would require definitive mismanagement.

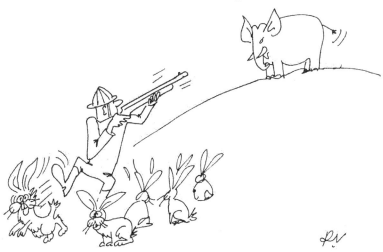

When none of the organizational shuffles put ADL back on the track, LaMantia ordered an increased emphasis on key-client management. This meant aiming primarily at any large and repetitive clients who spent a lot of money. It was hoped that by 2001 at least 25% of the company's new business would come from key-clients. The Company also defined and clarified the principal roles in a new matrix and implemented a company wide compensation plan to match it. Different reward measures were used for leaders and members of industry and functional practices, as well as for key-client managers, key-client team members, and market managers.

To get Company-wide support for these initiatives, ADL conducted an extensive training program in the application of the new strategy for leaders from all areas of the firm. In one three-day "jamboree" that was held in Charleston, South Carolina, at a cost of over a million dollars, LaMantia brought together 300 leaders of the firm from around the world. The cost of the meeting, combined with the disruption of work for senior managers had a significant negative effect on the year's operating profits.

The managers of ADL's European practice often disagreed with the business strategies coming from Cambridge. Already in 1984, they held a session in Vevey, Switzerland, with Derek Abel, who at the time was Dean at the Imede business school, leading the discussions. The purpose of the meeting was to get the European leadership to discuss and agree on the broad directions of the European strategy.

As the subsequent results showed, the strategy developed at the meeting was on the right track. While the situation in Cambridge deteriorated, ADL's European practice continued to be an area of strength, and the European managers gradually put pressure on Cambridge for greater participation in corporate management.

By the time LaMantia came in as President, the business in Europe had been growing comfortably. His appointment was not received with enthusiasm as LaMantia was seen as a kind of insecure introvert who was uneasy with Europeans. The morale in the European offices declined for the next few years, much of it rooted in the complexities of operating within a matrix of practice and office management.[10]

A second Vevey meeting, organized in 1990, was a good deal more chaotic than the previous one. To a large extent, it was used for venting of frustrations at a time when LaMantia was hectically organizing and reorganizing and seeking a more effective corporate identity. Having supported his efforts for several years, the Europeans were puzzled to see that many of the Cambridge initiatives tried to reinvent the wheels, which they had previously built in Europe. Because the number and the diversity of the participants at this meeting were greater, and the Europeans were frustrated not only with Cambridge management, but also with themselves, the meeting did not result in any explicit resolutions.

If 1997 was not a good year for ADL, 1998 was even worse. The only bright spot was Europe Consulting whose profits increased by 40%. Since the One-Company Management Platform had not produced the results that had been expected from it, LaMantia embarked on still another strategic initiative. Three innovation clus-

---

[10] To effectively deal with the financial and tax situation in each European country, the respective ADL offices were in charge of client work being done in the country. The practice centers, on the other hand, were located in different countries.

ters were launched with the following objectives.[11] Operational Performance Improvement would focus on "achieving breakthrough outcomes in bottom-line results". Product, Process and Service Innovation would focus on "achieving breakthrough outcomes in top-line growth." Corporate and Customer Innovation would focus on "achieving the strategic speed and flexibility to become an innovative enterprise."

The charter of the clusters was not to develop new products and services but to serve as frameworks for connecting the right mix of ADL competencies to clients' particular needs. Each cluster group included ADL personnel from a variety of practices and drew on ADL products and services to work for the client. In this way, the clusters were supposed to emphasize that ADL personnel were working together as teams rather than as individuals focusing on distinct dimensions of each case. In actuality, the cluster concept remained a mystery to many and did not produce the expected results.

As the strategies changed and grew in complexity from year to year, they did not provide the key to success in the increasingly competitive marketplace. The Company had lost sight of its principal competitive asset—the ability to combine technological expertise with management consulting. The value of the Company stock that had reached $134 in 1996, fell to $83. At the ADL Board meeting in December of 1998, LaMantia took the signal that he had to go.

In July 1999, LaMantia was replaced with Lorenzo Lamadrid[12] who again revamped the Company's organization. North American Consulting was unbundled into four basic business units.[13] Later in the year, the Management Consulting practice was reorganized, changing its focus from being geographically oriented to a single

---

[11] The clusters were the brainchild of David Robinson, then head of North American Consulting, who had come to ADL from Computer Sciences Corporation.
[12] Lamadrid had worked at the Boston Consulting Group but most of his business experience was in the utility industry as head of Western Resources International. He was credited with creating China's only Sino-foreign joint venture in electric power.
[13] These included Management Consulting; Technology and Product Development; Environmental, Health and Safety Consulting; and Public Sector Program Management.

Global Management Consulting entity. The idea was to emphasize key client management and develop a number of large global clients that spanned multiple geographic regions.

There was another major problem that Lamadrid had to face. Alan Friedman, the Senior VP for Human Resources had come to ADL from various management jobs at Philips N.V. and Wang Laboratories. He had been given a $10 million budget for the implementation of a system that would enable end-to-end service process optimization—from resource management to billing and revenue realization. The system had been very appealing to LaMantia since it integrated staff allocation, project management, cost collection and accounting. One was supposed to be able to run a professional services organization entirely by the numbers.

In fact, the system was best suited for companies that had many thousands of employees, such as information technology integrators and engineering firms. What Friedman did not recognize was that it would be very difficult to adapt such a system to the ADL culture where case leaders picked their own teams and did not follow a standardized project management system. As a result, the vendor ran into implementation problems and, by the time the progress with the system was about its midpoint, Friedman had spent $16 million without further authorization from the Board. ADL terminated the contract, sued the vendor, and recovered some of the funds.

In 1999, the European partners sent an explicit message to the ADL Board saying that they wanted a major voice in the company,[14] especially as ADL was doing very badly in the U.S. As a result, a new Global Leadership Team was established with a charter to manage the newly formed Global Management Practice. Composed primarily of senior managers from Europe Consulting, it came too late to have much impact on the failing North American Management Consulting business.

---

[14] In the mid-nineties, LaMantia asked all director/partners to buy substantial amounts of ADL stock. But the "partners" had no say whatsoever in how their investment in ADL was run. Some felt that LaMantia, like Magee before him, had become an absolute monarch. The carrier of the message, Roger Wippermann, was rudely ignored by management.

CHAPTER 9

The Fumbling Entrepreneurs

"Hardly anything is none of our business."[1]

ADL was the source of many interesting inventions, but it was not effective in exploiting them. Although it held about 3000 patents, only a few ever made any serious money for the Company. One of the earliest was the 1936 development of a method to obtain potable water on a tropical island with a minimum amount of fuel. Developed for the Navy, the prototype still could produce 175 pounds of fresh water with just one pound of fuel. Because the Navy then had no process for contracting with private industry for development, ADL developed the still at its own expense. Two years later, when the Navy issued a formal request for such a product, ADL won by a wide margin.

Since ADL did not have enough manpower to produce the stills in the required quantities, it licensed E. B. Badger & Sons to make them. Soon, the stills began to be installed on American submarines and deployed with Marine Corps task forces. ADL proudly claimed that, by the end of the war, enough still capacity was installed to supply ten million gallons of fresh water a day. The big money from the invention, however, was made by others.

Another opportunity arose after the war when Earl Stevenson identified the need for a method to liquefy helium more expeditiously than possible with existing processes. Professor Collins, a scientist at MIT, had built a prototype liquefier that brought temperatures

---

[1] Title of ADL's 1978 Annual Report

down to minus 456 degrees Fahrenheit, and Howard McMahon of ADL went about to improve it. At that time, there were only four laboratories in the world that had such capability and their equipment was home made and unreliable. The collaboration led to the development of the Collins helium cryostat that was ultimately installed in more than two hundred research laboratories around the globe. Instead of being a great commercial success for ADL, it paid off with a contract for engineering of the liquid fueling systems for the early ICBMs.

Aside from being unable to exploit commercial opportunities, ADL sometimes missed in advising its clients, as well. When IBM asked the Company to study whether it should invest in the newly emerging Xerox technology, ADL concluded that there would never be enough of a market for IBM to justify the expense. The Battelle Memorial Institute, on the other hand, was glad to take on the challenge and ended up with a rewarding chunk of Xerox stock.

From time to time, ADL had a vision of starting a new business. One idea was to make and sell helium liquefiers and related low-temperature engineering services. A large marketing program was set up that included direct sales, personalized direct mail, newsletters, calendars with boiling point conversion charts, news releases, exhibits at scientific gatherings, and ads in scientific journals. Scientists from ADL and MIT pitched in writing essays that could be handed out or mailed to prospects.

Hundreds of the cryostats and specialized derivatives were sold over the years, with the result that the field of cryogenics rose from a laboratory curiosity to where it is now commonplace in industrial, military, and scientific uses. Again, most of the profits went into pockets outside of ADL.

For many years, the rights to ADL's patents were almost always passed on to the clients. In 1958, ADL set up an invention management group—Arthur D. Little Enterprises, Inc. Its purpose was to help commercialize various technologies that were developed in-house, as well as by others, and share the proceeds with the inventors. The entity included only a few people and they did not have the experience to shepherd a technology into becoming a commercially viable product. Its primary function was to license technologies developed at ADL for commercialization by others, but a function for funding new ventures was added in the eighties. Any royalty income was reinvested in the unit's new equity projects.[2]

Among the successful technologies that ADL Enterprises worked with was a refrigeration compressor and an ink-jet printing process. The most rewarding to ADL, however, was an earlier patent for synthetic penicillin. It was granted to MIT in 1965, but ADL had a 44% stake in it. Eventually, this stake turned out to be worth $15 million.

ADL Enterprises received the most attention when it reached an agreement with a California inventor for a VCR technology named "Commercial Advance." The technology permitted fast-forwards

---

[2] The activities of ADL Enterprises reached a peak in 1989 when it achieved royalty income of $1.6 million—still a drop in the bucket when its potential was considered. Few of the equity investments proved to be profitable.

During the last few years of ADL's existence, the venture activities were extended beyond the area that was familiar to the Company. ADL invested $3 million in a Korean fund and committed $17 million to a European fund. After the bankruptcy, one million was recovered from the Korean venture. The European fund had never seen the money and it sued for breach of promise. The claim was settled in the bankruptcy court.

through commercials on video recordings of television programs and was licensed to eight major brands of VCR recorder manufacturers.

Going after computer technology

In the '60s, Dr. Bernhard Romberg, best known as Bernie, introduced computer technology to ADL. He was an imposing man six feet tall, already balding in his early thirties, and an organizational as well as a mathematics wizard. The project that truly put Bernie on the map was a large undertaking starting in 1966 for the Navy's Bureau of Ships. The idea was to turn architectural drawings into building schematics for battleships and to have an accuracy to the order of a quarter of an inch. The calculations at that time were based on a lofting process that connected points on a curved surface by bending a piece of wood through them and measuring where the intermediate points lay. The job of reducing the errors inherent in this process and to automate it was beyond the current state-of-the-art. It involved a large volume of data storage and retrieval problems, different formats and operations.

The Bureau of Ships case used every major method of computer science: graphics, mathematical modeling, multiple precision computation, and database list structures—all stored and retrieved and operated on in a new computer language. The system extracted, rearranged and replaced its data in batches of hundreds or thousands of points at a time. These were then re-organized into transverse or longitudinal bulkheads or decks or hulls. It carved bulkheads into plates by rules using artificial intelligence. It plotted assembly drawings for pen plotters or CRTs and punched out numerical tapes to drive flame cutters.

The project was so complex and required so many different parts that the schedule charts necessary to run it had to be huge and updated frequently. This was the first time that ADL produced such management data on the computer. Bernie used to modify the charts on the airplane while returning from client meetings.

When he got back to the office, someone would punch up the cards to re-run the charts and mail them to the contract officer. One time Bernie had a major revision to be done over the weekend and asked another ADLer who was familiar with that program to help him. When the fellow balked because he had reserved the Saturday to mow the lawn at his Carlisle house, Bernie picked up the tab for having somebody else do the mowing.

Bernie believed that the client expected not only quality but also a certain amount of quantity in the delivered work. In one case, he approached a staff member who wrote his reports in longhand and, since he had been trained as a journalist, wrote reports that were very concise and to the point. Bernie thought that the reports should be longer. "But I have already written all there is," the staff member protested. "Then why don't you try dictating," Bernie suggested. The staff member followed his suggestion and, indeed, his reports turned out longer than before.

The programmers who worked on the project had an exhilarating time. The undertaking was so massive that all preliminary testing was done with a sample of the data. A real ship that was being built in Quincy Shipyard was used as a test model and all plans were developed in parallel by the computer and by the traditional naval architecture methods. When ADL was about three years into the project and running daily tests of the programs there were so many boxes of cards and so many tapes and disks to move between ADL and the computer center in Cambridge that Bernie hired a fellow whose sole job was to do that. The fellow attended the program runs to see that all instructions were followed, recorded any problems, and brought it all back in the form of hundreds of pages of printout. Even with a large freight dolly, it required a vigorous physical specimen who attended to the last detail and quickly picked up all the staff idiosyncracies.

Bernie recognized that programmers, like engineers, tend to fine-tune their products long after they have been completed. To keep the project within budget, he introduced a very simple but effective system. As soon as a programmer completed a task, it was locked away in a drawer, and no changes were permitted unless proven necessary.

Although the system was developed by the Navy with the intention that it would provide a modern tool to the ship-building industry, it did not work out that way. The shipbuilding companies wanted to build their own tools rather than use the ones developed by the Navy. They hired away ADLs naval architects as fast as they could, they built their own tools, and never used the ones that ADL had designed. After the system was delivered to the Navy, no commercial company ever ran it.

Another flagship case led by Bernie Romberg was the back office trading system for the New York Stock Exchange. This was a first of its kind. Bernie bid on it just before the new programming language PL1 came out and ADL wanted to use it for its expected superior performance and functionality. Since nobody knew how well the language would perform, some risk was involved. Bernie, however, felt that with the experience on the Bureau of Ships program behind them, ADL could bet that PL1 could be made to work.

Because of the genius of Bernie Romberg and the conservative approach to the New York Stock Exchange case, everybody was a winner when PL1 was delivered and tests showed that it would do the job. Still, it was a big undertaking to process all the buys and sells and update the quotes at the Exchange in real-time. Since the only time ADL could test the program was in the middle of the night, Bernie was there making sure every-thing went smoothly. At one point, the Chairman of the Exchange came through and found Bernie sitting at the key-punch updating somebody's code. He was thoroughly shocked and thundered "We are not paying you to key-punch." Bernie calmly stood up and politely looming over him said "No, you are paying me to run this project and do what most needs doing. And right at this particular minute, this is what most needs doing."

These were the days when executives really did not know how to type. The idea of one typing was unthinkable and keypunching was even lower. But Bernie knew what was important and when the best thing for the team was for him to keypunch, he keypunched. He also arranged for food. His employees praised him as a terrific leader because he knew how to motivate a team. Everybody was expected to know what was going on, everybody contributed, and everybody was valued.

ADL Systems

Bernie Romberg was not only a successful case manager but also a budding entrepreneur. He was able to convince John Magee, who had recently become the president, that ADL could compete in the growing programming business. Bernie started out quietly with a unit of programmers within ADL, but to take advantage of a different overhead cost structure and contract requirements, he pushed and got the light to set up a subsidiary—ADL Systems, Inc. He wanted to go after the growing software development business that had been a lucrative activity for such companies as Arthur Andersen.

While this venture was in a growing and promising field, bright and ambitious consultants rather than business people managed it. Although they had successfully worked on lucrative government projects, they had little experience in the commercial marketplace. Bernie was installed as president of ADL Systems, but some of the staff soon grew to dislike him. However, while they thought that he was inflexible and some-times even tyrannical, they recognized that he was a good salesman. They made an effort to get the subsidiary into major systems projects but never learned to manage them profitably.

A major business area for ADL Systems (ADLS) was envisioned in the Medicaid Management Information System (MMIS) projects. The federal government supported them, but required each state to up-grade its system. Despite considerable competition from such orga-nizations as Ross Perot, ADLS won the contracts for MMIS projects in a number of states. It turned out, however, that doing business in the highly competitive software business was very different from the professional services that Bernie and his team was used to.

To support the MMIS business, a big investment was made in buying the Delphi Company that had contacts with federal and state authorities. The contracts were usually fixed-price and depended on change orders to be profitable. Differences of opinion between the consultants and the clients resulted in many lawsuits. While ADL Systems never lost a single lawsuit, the activity reflected badly on the parent company.

For example, a difficult situation developed in the State of Illinois where the client demanded various enhancements that were not specified by the contract. It had been ADL's practice to always please the client and address such changes in the expectation that in the end they would be compensated. In Illinois, however, the estimated cost to complete the project increased significantly from month to month, and there was no contractual provision for covering the extra costs.

When the seriousness of the situation became known, John Magee himself went down to meet the client and ADL assigned an executive to oversee the situation. It was concluded that it would be impossible to continue and that the contract should be terminated as soon as possible. Although ADLS expected that the client would sue, the Company felt that it could successfully defend itself and, furthermore, ADL thought that the client would need continued ADLS support to operate the system. When the contract was terminated, the client still owed ADLS $2 million that it refused to pay. For a number of reasons, not least of which being the fact that in the '70s software projects represented a complex issue that was not fully understood by the courts, the suit was not immediately filed. Time passed as the ADLS lawyers and the Illinois attorney general's office juggled for positions. Finally, Bernie saved the day and ADLS got its money after a junior member of the attorney general's staff was wined and dined at Acorn Park.

One of the ADLS projects was to design the accounting and inventory control system for the United Shoe Machinery Corporation.

The product did not meet the promised response times and the client sued for breach of warranty. ADLS went to trial by arguing that it had exercised its best efforts, as stated in the contract, and therefore the risks of a poor performance fell on the client. The Massachusetts Appeals Court, however, held that ADLS had taken on the complete responsibility for the system and the poor response time was a design defect. Even the fact that USM employees had worked closely with the development of the system did not excuse ADLS from its warranty obligations.

ADLS also had problems with a subcontractor who had performed work outside the contractual scope and wanted to get paid for it. When ADLS refused, the subcontractor sued. ADLS filed a counter suit. A settlement was eventually reached, but it emphasized to ADL that doing business in the software marketplace was not the same as management consulting.

Bernie was eventually forced out, but Howard Morrison who replaced him, got into an even bigger mess. The package that ADL Systems offered to clients included minicomputers, the value of which was booked as sales in advance. The package was dependent on the name of ADL, and the parent Company was concerned that any system failure would reflect badly on its reputation. Finally, the minicomputers turned out not to be as capable as expected. This work in a highly competitive area of business resulted in overruns and even lawsuits from dissatisfied clients. John Magee came under criticism from the ADL board and ADLS was absorbed back into the company. Thus, another brave attempt at ADL entrepreneurship met its usual fate.

CHAPTER 10

Into the Wide World

During an assignment in Taiwan to evaluate a planned fertilizer plant, three staff members were driven to the proposed site in a jeep. As they approached the site, a worker jumped up waving his hands and shouting in Chinese. Then the ADLers noticed dynamite sticks on the ground just a few feet ahead. With no time to back up the jeep, the consultants jumped out and ran for their lives amid a shower of rocks.

International work had been a mainstay of ADL's work since 1916 when Dr. Little was invited to undertake a survey of Canada's natural resources. As a result of this study, he opened an office In Montreal. It was very successful and generated 165 reports within seven months. However, history shows a fragile record for ADL's Canadian activities. The Montreal office did not last long, and in more recent years ADL was represented in Canada by a lone individual in Toronto. To the people in Cambridge, it was just another foreign country and not a very exciting one at that.

ADL's international operations really took off in the late fifties. The operations research staff had done some work for clients in London and this led to seminars at Oxford and Versailles. The Operations Research section opened a small project office in London. One of the interesting projects at the time was an investigation of the loss of two airplanes and key engineering staff by British Aircraft. When the first airplane suddenly dropped to the ground, the engineers climbed into the second one to replicate the flight. It crashed the same way killing everyone aboard. The technical reason was quickly determined—at a certain angle of descent the flaps cut off airflow to the stabilizers and caused the aircraft to free-fall. ADL's assignment was to find the clues to the organizational problems that led to the second crash and loss of key personnel.

When ADL first started opening offices in Europe, it sent over Americans who hired local personnel. These people sometimes felt abandoned, so whenever anybody from Cambridge was traveling in Europe, on business or otherwise, they were encouraged to stop by the European offices. This was interesting, but it was not clear that it helped any business purpose. On one occasion, a Cambridge staff member arrived at the Brussels office early in the morning and walked into the office of Harland Riker whom he had met before and assumed that he would be remembered. Indeed, Riker received him very enthusiastically, but after they had sat down, he pulled out a piece of paper and started to talk about a job application. He had mistaken the Cambridge colleague for an applicant he was expecting for an interview.

The initial thrust of the European operations was to represent American companies seeking to expand their export trade. Cambridge staff members moved to Europe with little or no knowledge of the local language or customs. This changed over the next ten years as European companies wanted to expand their export business, and there were few local consulting companies they could turn to. ADL realized that the expatriates were not best suited for dealing with these clients and adopted a policy of hiring local candidates for the key positions.

Staffing the European offices with locals was a two-edged sword. Clearly, they were better equipped to bring in new business and complete assignments with occasional help from Cambridge. However, the locals felt they did not have the same financial opportunities as the Cambridge staff and were likely to leave for other jobs. This was because, for a variety of legal technicalities, they were not members of the MDT retirement fund. They belonged to their own retirement programs that were not viewed as desirable as the MDT. This eventually led to serious crises that required compromises on the part of ADL management, but it also set up the conditions that led to the acquisition of parts of ADL by the European managers at the bankruptcy sale.

Much of the time, the situation in Europe was difficult because leads originating in a given country were usually given to the respective ADL office even if it had questionable capabilities of carrying it out. When tensions developed between Cambridge and Europe, Hamilton James, a senior executive with international experience, was put in charge to level the situation. When Charlie Kensler came in as Chief Professional Officer, James was replaced by Harland Riker, who had shown success in the Middle East. But although Riker hired the best people he could find, the profits lagged.[1]

In principle, ADL was involved in two types of international operations. One was foreign assignments carried out by Cambridge staff. The other was work sold and implemented by the staff of the foreign offices. Theoretically, each case would be staffed with the most qualified people, whether they were from Cambridge or from abroad. Actually, because of travel costs and office politics, this was not always done.

Many Cambridge staff members were interested to work on cases in exotic locations, but as the organization matured, such opportunities became limited. Leadership of most of the foreign cases was taken over by foreign offices that wanted to use their own people. One ruse sometimes used was to staff the case with independent contractors who did good work but did not want to become permanent employees. This set up a situation where the local case leader could potentially get a kickback.

In Saudi Arabia, ADL had set up the Saudi Consulting House within the Ministry of Industry. Staffed with the brightest professionals locally available, it performed advisory functions as well as some industry regulatory functions for the Saudi government. For ADL,

---

[1] Some in Cambridge blamed the poor profit margins on insufficient cost control. Actually, it was not a matter of control but rather a different approach of expensing overhead activities in Europe. Reflecting the local tax situation, European practices provided various fringe benefits that would not be commonly accepted in the United States.

this turned out to be a very useful move. The practice in Saudia Arabia called for all foreign work to be sponsored by a local company or individual who then received a given percentage fee. Finding sponsors with sufficient influence in granting contracts was the problem faced by every foreign company trying to do business. Through the Saudi Consulting House, ADL had direct access to key government officials and this was accomplished without paying the customary fees.

ADL also had several staff members working as advisors to high-level Saudi officials. The ADL advisor to the Minister of Industry even wrote his speeches. Until 1992, ADL had worked on the economic plans for Saudi Arabia, as well as other large contracts. By this time, however, interest in such projects and the flow of money had decreased and ADL attempted to sell consulting services to

other Saudi businesses. The composition of the local staff changed from expatriates to the brightest professionals from the Arab world. One of the largest private sector projects at that time dealt with gas station management, but ADL lost out when it came up for renewal. In the end, ADL's work consisted mostly of feasibility studies, and all activity was discontinued by 2000.

In Brazil, the ADL office had a problem with a telex line that was frequently breaking down. Since telephone conversations to Cambridge were very expensive, it was critical to improve the telex service. One day, a Brazilian construction worker showed up at the office and said he knew about the telex problem and could fix it for a thousand dollars in cash. After considering the proposal, the office manager dipped into petty cash. From then on, the telex line ran without interruptions.

The Manila venture

The first big international case for ADL started in 1969 in the Philippines. By the time it was finished, fifty-six ADLers had worked on it, and the final report filled five hardcover volumes. The contract from the World Bank and United Nations asked ADL to do a transportation survey of South East Asia. For the very first time, ADL would have to send half a dozen personnel and their families for a two-year stint in Manila. Since it would mean losing contact with the fast-growing activities in Cambridge, few ADLers were anxious to make the move. In addition, everybody was concerned about the extremely hot climate and security risks in the Philippines.

ADL had no experience in sending people to countries other than Europe for any extended time and there was no administrative structure to handle the problems associated with the move. After surveying the types of incentives other companies offered to their personnel, ADL came up with a package that sounded very attractive. The consultants would receive foreign assignment bonuses, their household goods would be shipped and returned at the client's expense, children would get to attend American schools, and residences would be provided. Because of the UN relationship, the personnel would receive certain diplomatic privileges, such as monthly allotments of duty-free liquor, ability to buy automobiles at diplomatic rates, etc.

The first problem occurred within a few weeks after the ADLers arrived in Manila. The client made the initial payment—a six-figure amount that needed to be deposited. However, since ADL was not registered in the Philippines, it was impossible to open an account in its name. The administrators in Cambridge did not know what to do and asked for more time. In the meantime, the staff needed money to cover expenses in Manila. Somebody found out that, as an interim measure, one could open an account in his own name and deposit the Company check without any questions being asked. If the administrators in Cambridge had known that, they would have gone out of their minds—but it worked.

The next problem was that, after arriving in Manila, everybody lived at the Intercontinental Hotel. The villas had been rented, the maids and drivers had been hired, but there was, as yet, no furniture. It was sitting in containers waiting to be cleared by the Philippine customs. Inquiries through the official channels led nowhere, as the customs officials were expecting bribes. In the meantime, the wives and children were growing increasingly bored and frustrated with living in the hotel. The situation was finally resolved when ADL hired a young local lady as a facilitator. With a pad of dollar bills in her purse she went to have coffee with the customs officials. The containers were released the following day and the only remaining problem was how to account for the missing money to Cambridge.

The project office was located in the prestigious Manila suburb of Makati, and the consultants lived in luxurious villas in the adjoining fenced-in villages. As appropriate, the fanciest villa was rented for the project director. He could dive into a small pool in a corner of his bedroom and emerge in a large pool in the garden. Given his age, it was questionable whether he ever tried it.

Although the villas were within walking distance from the office, the heat and humidity prevented the consultants from walking. By the time they got used to the climate a few months later, they had become accustomed to taking the car if just for a few blocks. Many joined the exclusive Manila Polo Club that had an Olympic size pool, good food and drink, as well as social functions where one could meet local executives and other expatriates.

The consultants traveled frequently to Indonesia, Singapore, Malaysia, Thailand and Vietnam, and their diplomatic visas gave them many advantages. Stopovers in Hong Kong gave the opportunity to stock up on photographic and electronics gear and bring them in through the Philippine customs without inspection. Every other month, they could sign up for a duty-free liquor shipment. The allocations were very generous, and unless one was used to giving frequent parties, he could use the extra bottles of scotch like cash in acquiring hand-carved chests and other objects.

ADL had sent over a senior executive to serve as the project director. To the people in Cambridge, it seemed like an easy assignment for somebody who was close to retirement. The project team occupied one floor of a high-rise in the Makati business center while the project director had an office several floors higher among executives of the local partner. He seldom came down to visit the team, and since the executive floor was air conditioned to a brisk 65F, staff members avoided going up there so as not to catch a cold.

One day the project administrator was riding in the director's car when the driver surprised him by asking how much scotch he consumed each day. When the administrator hesitated, the driver volunteered that the director drank a bottle each day. Since the administrator's tasks included approving the staff expense accounts, he looked into the report submitted by the director. Sure enough, there was an item for several cases of scotch used for "representation." The administrator justifiably inquired about the nature of the "representation," but did not get an answer. Soon thereafter, he received a message from Cambridge that the director would send in his expense reports himself without a local review.

Actually, it was not difficult to notice where the scotch went. At noon, the director usually had lunch with his wife at the same hotel frequented by the staff members. Sometimes he would slurp over his meal, and once he brought quite a bit of attention to himself when he dropped his dentures on the table.

Aside from causing such embarrassing situations and missing out on the details of the project, the director also was insensitive to the local customs. Sometimes, he would show up for a meeting thirty minutes late, and at other times he would embarrass client officials by addressing them by their first name. The staff soon realized that the project director was ineffective, embarrassing, and interfered with the work getting done as planned. The deputy director and a few conspirators put their necks on the line and sent a letter to Cambridge requesting that the director be replaced. Based on previous experience with Cambridge, they figured that they might be fired for their actions. This time, however, a senior executive promptly came out for a visit, and soon thereafter the project had a new director.[2]

Another major crisis occurred when the client learned that the staff members had received salary increases after the contract was signed. The Indian who was the client's representative on the project insisted that the contract did not permit it and stated that they would refuse to pay. The extra salaries totaled several hundred thousand dollars over the length of the project and would have wiped out any profit. This news caused a flap in Cambridge, and nobody knew what to do. The lawyers agreed that Cambridge had made a mistake in negotiating the contract terms and did not see any way to avoid the overrun.

By that time, the project administrator had been in Manila long enough to know that there was always more than one way to skin a cat. Having learned that the bank official in charge of manpower planning was a Dane, he figured he might feel some relationship to a Latvian like himself. He invited the bank officer over to his house—they had a few beers, looked over the contract, and came to the agreement that, no matter what the paper said, the salary increases were reasonable. The project director was so pleased with this outcome that he recom-mended the administrator for a special award, but Cambridge never acknowledged it.

---

[2] There was a slight delay because the Cambridge visitor became violently ill from some local shrimp he ate upon his arrival and needed time to recover.

The relationships with the client sometimes bordered on the absurd. For example, their auditors noticed that the ADL consultants were being reimbursed for warehousing household items in Massachusetts. Naturally, the ADLers had brought along only the necessary goods, leaving the rest in storage until the end of the project. This was not in line with the Asian bank's procedures. Their consultants were permitted to bring in up to two containers of goods, but there were no provisions for paying storage costs. The result was that the ADLers had all the old furniture and, in one case, a pile of fireplace wood shipped to the Philippines at the bank's expense. Some used the oppor-tunity to benefit from low labor costs and had their furniture refinished before returning it to the States.

Business customs in Manila were different from those ADLers were familiar with, including the importance of bribes. While ADL had a strict policy against paying bribes or commissions, these practices were widely followed by other companies. For example, the comptroller of an English tobacco company was always looking for off-the-books dollars to bribe Philippine officials and was willing to pay a high peso rate to get them. At the same time, the ADLers received their salary in dollars and needed to buy pesos for local use. One staff member met the Englishman at a party and soon had a lucrative money exchange going, supplying his colleagues with cheap pesos. The scheme broke up when another ADLer met the same Englishman and found that he could get an even better rate by dealing with him directly.

Especially challenging to the Americans was the fact that Asians place great importance on saving face and often do not give clear answers if they cannot be positive. For example, an ADLer took his broken stereo receiver to a shop to be fixed. He checked back from time to time, only to be told that the repairs would take another week. When he finally lost patience, the repairman conceded that he did not know how to fix the machine.

One ADLer traveled twice to Saigon to collect statistical information from the Chief of Police. Each time upon arrival, he found that the meeting was cancelled because the official was off in some other country attending a conference. Since the conferences had been scheduled far ahead, it was clear that the meeting date had been intentionally timed to avoid a face to face encounter. The reason, most probably, was that the official did not want to admit that he did not have the requested data.

Guessing what the client wanted the consultants to do or not to do was also part of doing business. In 1970, the Manila staff and their wives planned a Christmas party to which various officials of the bank were to be be invited. The client executive, a Chinese, said there could be no party. The Americans could not figure out whether it had to do with Christmas or some feature of the proposed party. On a whim, somebody suggested that the women should be excluded. With this new provision, the Chinese executive readily agreed to have the party.

Manila had several markets where the conditions were extremely unsanitary; ADLers included some of them on sightseeing tours for visitors from Cambridge. One of the worst was a meat section where carcasses lay piled up on wooden tables in the 90 heat.[3] One of the visitors who had courageously suffered through the tour subsequently flew to Hong Kong. When he arrived at the hotel and opened his suitcase, he was nearly felled over by a terrible stench. On further examination, he found the source of the odor was the shoes he had worn to the Manila meat market.

Aside from the heat, earthquakes, and tornadoes that one could get used to, the consultants were also exposed to a trigger-happy society. This was brought too close to home one afternoon when a report came in that the director's driver had shot somebody during his lunch hour. Nobody had even known that he carried a gun. The report further stated that the consultants should watch out since the victim's friends were out gunning for the driver.

---

[3] This was probably the reason why most Filipino meat dishes involved long cooking and were often enhanced with anchovies. For the traditional adobo, meat was boiled in vinegar before going to the frying pan.

Amid all the confusion, the driver returned from his lunch break as if nothing had happened. The police had cleared him because the victim—or his body—had disappeared on the way to the hospital. While nobody dared to stand anywhere near him, he insisted that he wanted to continue as the driver. It took more than a month's salary to negotiate him out the door.

One of the staff members had a close call when he had temporarily moved into the house of the U.S. Embassy doctor. Late one evening, after the maids had retired, there was a knock on the door. It was the wife of a Danish subcontractor who was known to have marital difficulties. She was quite upset, so the ADLer set her at the bar and mixed her a martini. About that time, he heard strange noises on the roof. This was nothing unexpected, as the house had the reputation of being haunted, and that was the reason the maids always left before dark. When the noises continued, however, he went outside and found somebody hiding in the bushes and throwing rocks on the roof. It was the woman's husband—quite embarrassed and trying to hide a gun behind his back.

"Good to see you," the ADLer told him. "You can take your wife home before she gets drunk."

Other projects

Work abroad was the subject of many curious incidents that required imagination. One of the earliest occurred in 1954 when Mike Michaelis represented ADL at the First International Conference on Atomic Energy, held under the auspices of the U.N. in Geneva. The U.N. recognized him only as an "observer" because, lacking US citizenship, he could not be on the U.S. Delegation and, having left the U.K. three years earlier, the Brits no longer recognized him either. Observer status meant that he could attend all sessions, but timely news of where and what was going to happen was difficult to get. Yet, that was important if he was to participate fully and thus benefit ADL's emerging nuclear consulting service.

Michaelis noticed that there were wooden boxes on the wall on the ground floor of the Palais de Nations, where the meetings were held. They were marked with delegation names, from "Albania" to "Zanzibar" and beyond to alphabet soup such as UNESCO, WHO, etc. They were filled daily with all kinds of useful information. There was one box still unmarked. Michaelis attached to it the designation "ADL / US2" (the latter portion to be read phonetically). From then on, all conference news, invitations to delegate receptions, etc. flowed into that box as into all the others.

Another large international project was the reorganization of the Egyptian National Telecommunications Company in the seventies. About a dozen ADLers were in residence in Cairo and others came for short assignments from the US and Europe. Although the consultants preferred to stay in smaller hotels, everybody knew the Sheraton because of its casino. The word was that the Egyptians had not yet learned to fleece their customers, and the chances for winning were much better than at similar establishments elsewhere in the world.

One afternoon, as an ADLer and an American visitor were walking past the hotel, the visitor had a quick idea. "Would you mind if we stop for a few minutes at the casino?"

The visitor bought a few chips, proceeded to the gaming tables, and in less than five minutes emerged with several hundred dollars. "That is all I promised for my wife," he remarked casually to the astonished ADLer. "We can go now."

Communications with clients outside the United States were sometimes difficult and, despite the best efforts, often did not yield the expected results. This could happen even in an English speaking country like Canada. Prior to a presentation in Winnipeg, Manitoba, the client's secretary was requested to provide a room with a slide projector. She phoned the facilities manager at her company and told him "We will be needing a room with a projector for the A.D. Little people who will be coming from Cambridge." Ten minutes later, the exasparated facilities manager called back and declared, "I am afraid we have no room that can accomodate eighty little people."

Foreign assignments sometimes involved unexpected dangers. After a week in Brazil, a pair of ADLers was on the way to the airport when their taxi hit some railroad tracks and broke an axle. Fuel poured from the damaged gas tank and, within seconds, the car was in flames. While the consultants were fortunate to escape, they lost all their personal belongings, as well as the case reports.

Sometimes, seasoned consultants could use the foreign situation to play a joke on their less experienced colleagues. When a new executive was brought in to develop the program management market, he was not well received by staff members who had not been consulted and felt they had this area under control. The tension increased when the new man announced he would make a site visit to a client in Brazil.

The case involved a large new blast furnace of national importance and the client was worried that there could be glitches in its start-up. The new executive had rarely been out of the United States and, furthermore, he was not familiar with the steel industry. Reflecting on his own experience, he suggested to the client that he should imitate the U.S. space effort and build a small scale pilot plant to test everything beforehand. But how do you build a smaller blast furnace just to test it? Our seasoned consultants wanted to crawl into the ground.

That evening, the ADLers retired to the local hotel. The weather was stifingly hot. Although the rooms had air conditioners, the controls were located out of sight in the drawer of the night table. Soon, the consultants noticed that the new executive was suffering from the heat in his room, but was not aware there was an air conditioner. Nobody told him until he stumbled on the controls a day later.

As far as the blast furnace was concerned, it was started up on schedule with the pomp and circumstance necessary to impress the participating government officials. The only glitch was that the ladle cars had not arrived and the first cast had to be poured on the tracks below. It took months of hard work to cut up the cold steel and reprocess it.

The further one moved away from Cambridge, the more likely were the problems of misunderstanding. When ADL had a project team living in the Phillipines, time was needed to get used to the local pronounciation of the English language. One staff member had a startling encounter when his maid returned from her annual health examination.

"What did the doctor say?" he asked.

"He said everyting is good, but I should brush my teets."

After a pause, the staff member realized that the maid was talking about her teeth.

The situation was even more embarassing for a staff member in Brazil whose car had a flat tire on this way to the office. He was due for a meeting, so he asked the secratary to call somebody to fix the tire—known in Portugese as a "pneu." In the middle of the meeting, the secretary stuck her head in the door and announced in her accented English "Mr. Jones, the boy is here to blow your pneus."

Despite all of ADL's international work, it seemed that the staff in Cambridge never really understood the cultural idiosyncracies in client countries. In 1993, an article in ADL's employee newspaper *Little Paper* featured award winning case teams where the consultants were pictured in funny poses. In one of the pictures, a very serious, young and bespectacled ADL consultant was seen showing the thumb-index finger gesture. In Cambridge that meant OK, but in Brazil it was equivalent to raising the middle finger. To make things even worse, the young man was holding a measuring tape in his other hand. Obviously, this caused a laughing riot in ADL's Brazilian office.

Misunderstandings were an almost daily occurence at the ADL Management Education Institute that was attended primarily by foreign executives. To help the students get adjusted to a foreign country, faculty and other staff members were encouraged to invite them to their homes.

An African student visited an ADL family living in a town house in Cambridge. After a pleasant dinner, as the guest was departing, the hosts wished him "Good bye and take care." The student returned to his apartment very agitated and complained to his fellow students: "If they live in such a dangerous area, they should at least have accompanied me to the bus."

In 1991, the foreign students were asked to describe how they saw the process of becoming an American. These were some of their comments:

"I will buy the fastest food I can get, and I will eat very slowly because I watch TV during the meals."

"As an American, I will have an answering machine, too. The outgoing message will promise that I will call back as soon as possible, but it won't be possible soon. If I answer the phone as an exception, I will say that I can't talk now because I have a long distance call on the other line and that I will call back as soon as possible, but it won't be possible soon."

"As an American, I will always be concerned about my health. I won't eat anything but health food until I get ill."

CHAPTER 11

The Secret Sex Life

As representatives of America's most prestigious consulting firm, ADLers were serious, fairly formal and gave the appearance of being happily married. In fact, the time consultants spent traveling exerted strong pressures on family life and foreign assignments were even more demanding. ADLers were not much different from others in their generation, but they often handled things differently. One fellow was so intent on keeping his marital woes secret that he sought to establish residence in Nevada and get a divorce there. When an opportune case came along, he stretched the assignment out to four weeks during which he lived in a hotel in Reno. When he returned, he was happily unmarried.

While at times there were a romances between staff members and affairs between staff members and secretaries, these were few and far apart. This does not mean that consultants were not interested in the opposite sex. Walking along the Charles river in Cambridge on a sunny afternoon one might recognize a colleague lounging in the grass with his secretary.

One particular, very solid, conservative family man was known to look for women whenever he arrived in a new city. He was working on a case in Brazil when the clients took charge by inviting the ADL team to a famous brothel in a village outside Rio. This was not unusual—Brazilians are very proud of their brothels and will gladly show them off to visitors. As the consultants drank beer in the center of the old building, the clients carefully explained the room arrangements with their various price ranges. The curtains along the wall, they explained, were for "quickies." You could get five-dollar service while standing up. As the glasses emptied and the consultants got up to leave, their conservative colleague unexpectedly bolted. "Excuse me a minute," he said, disappearing behind the curtains. "I just want to try a quickie."

Involvement with Brazilian women could end up unpleasantly. One of the consultants who traveled regularly to Belo Horizonte struck it up with a woman who promptly fell in love with him. When he arrived, she awaited him with flowers, and when he left, she followed him to the airport, full of tears at the departure gate, begging him not to leave. "Don't get involved!" he advised his colleagues. "The trouble isn't worth it."

Although ADLers did not usually get personally involved with the secretaries of clients, some relationships did develop, especially in foreign assignments. In one instance, a consultant was so impressed by the attention he received from the client's secretary that he took her out to dinner. At the end of a pleasant evening, she started to hum a popular song, something like "take me home with you." The consultant promptly parted from her, and their business relationship was never the same.

The advice not to get involved was apparently forgotten by two consultants who were sitting in a cafe in Ipanema when a pretty local girl came over to ask for the time. Before they knew it, they were joined by three older Brazilian women whose objective seemed to be to go to dinner and dance late into the night with somebody on an expense account.

With nothing better to do, the consultants reluctantly agreed. It was decided that the women would go home for their afternoon siesta and wait to be picked up at eight. Keeping his promise, one of the consultants showed up at the apartment at the agreed time, but quickly realized that it was a million dollar "pad" just steps away from the beach and anybody living there would have extravagant taste.[1] The pretty young girl had disappeared, but the older women were busy prepping themselves up for a big night on the town. Alone in the living room, the ADLer quickly calculated the potential expense and the case work waiting for him in the morn-

---

[1] Since divorce in Brazil is nearly impossible, middle-aged women occupy many of the luxury apartments along Ipanema beach, having received them upon separation from their rich husbands.

ing. He quietly tiptoed to the door and snuck out. Out on the street, he waited to forewarn his colleague of the trap. As it turned out, the other ADLer had already sized up the situation and had left his friend to handle it all on his own.

Another ADLer tells of a highly respected engineer with whom he occasionally worked on a case. The two of them traveled frequently to Florida and shared a rental car. Their dinner conversations were dull, usually about some aspect of the case or business development in general. One day the engineer asked to take the rental car that evening to do an errand. Since the other consultant had no other plans, he agreed. Later, when he woke up in the middle of the night and glanced out the window, he noticed that his colleague had not yet returned. The next morning at breakfast, he asked him about it.

"Oh, the trip turned out to be much longer than I expected," was the answer. "You see, I collect antique cars, and I went to see one I saw advertised. It turned out to be a long trip, and I got back very late." The ADLer did not remember exactly when and how the conversation turned to women, but he eventually learned that there was no antique car, but a woman the colleague had met in the hotel bar. A lot of mysterious episodes suddenly fell into place. He learned that the colleague often crashed hotel parties and even had made love to a stewardess in the toilet of a London-bound flight.

"I do have one problem," the fellow confessed. "When I go into a bar, I take off my wedding ring, but the mark is left behind. There doesn't seem to be any way to get away from it."

The colleague then shared a non-engineering solution with him. "See this college ring?" he showed his hand. "I bought it for just that reason. Nobody can tell there was a wedding band there before." From then on, the two were good friends, and the ADLer could count on being asked to join cases that came along the engineer's way.

When ADL had a project office in Manila, one case team member constantly complained about noise and interruptions. As a solution, he was given his own office where he could close the door, but the movement outside the glass wall bothered him as well. He was so hard to live with that management for a time considered replacing him, however his knowledge of the subject was so good that they could not do without him.

One day a middle-aged Englishwoman walked in from the street and right into the office of the project manager. "I am stranded here in Manila, and I cannot afford a place to stay," she said. "Would any of the men here like me to move in with them?"

The manager's first impulse was to shove her out the door, but then he thought of the frustrated team member and took her over to meet him. The following day, the Englishwoman moved in with the consultant, and there were no more complaints from him again.

Then there was the fellow from the Cambridge office who got stuck between flights in Tokyo. He checked into a hotel, then went for a walk wondering how to spend a boring weekend. Somehow, while looking at a window display, he struck up with a young woman who spoke fairly good English. She turned out to be an off-duty geisha. She invited him to her home and he never returned to the hotel until the time for his flight on Monday.

The mens room was often a good place to start business transactions. One such across-the-bowls conversation led me to the North of Canada to the site of a fire-damaged processing plant. The case leader was a ranking engineer and we were to be joined in Canada by an expert from Texas with whom he had worked for many years. I was warned that he would be flying in with his own airplane and would show off as a serious ladies man.

The Texan was genuine with a tall hat and cowboy boots. The remote town where we stayed had just one motel and a bar. As we sat down for dinner, my colleagues started off on girl stories and the Texan flirted with the waitress and any other women within reach. I joined in and pretty soon had established contact with two Lithuanian girls at the next table. The case leader excused himself to go to bed, so I suggested to the Texan that he and I join the girls. Much to my surprise, he was suddenly sleepy as well.

The following day after work, I had a telephone call from the Texan. He had some questions about the work we had done that day and asked me if I could come over to his room to discuss it. His door was ajar and as I opened it, I found him posing with a cigar in the hand and one leg up on a chair. I stopped in my tracks, turned and was out in a second. Except for his hat and boots, the Texan was stark naked.

After this incident I gave some thought to the case leader and came to the conclusion that he was gay. I had noticed that he always talked about his friends of an unspecified gender, but I had not made the connection. Now I wondered if he invited me to the case because of my blue eyes.

My encounter with the Texan had unexpected consequences. Back in the office, the case leader declared he was unhappy with my report and found various reasons why he could not work with me any more. From a most useful project management expert I had suddenly turned into a liability.

Since I had an impeccable reputation, this incident did not have any effect on me. However, a similar experience did not turn out so well for one of my colleagues. As in the incident with me, the gay case leader declared after a trip that my colleague's report was completely wrong. He did not stop with that, but urged the section head to keep the consultant away from any of his clients. This was a serious charge made at a time when ADL was painfully experiencing its first staff reduction. The poor fellow got axed.

CHAPTER 12

The Financial Fiasco

The financial crisis that brought ADL down was not its first. Much earlier, at the end of 1921, ADL books showed a net loss and consideration was given to dissolving the company and distributing its assets. The motion was defeated by the Board, but the following year staff salaries were cut by ten percent, and Dr. Little took a 15% cut himself. The Memorial Drive building was mortgaged.

For the remainder of the twenties, ADL managed to show a modest profit, but it depended on a few major clients. It could have tried to diversify, but instead the Company increased the emphasis on serving the existing clients. The idea was to make them so dependent that they could not afford to do without ADL's services. This did not always work, and as the client interests changed, so did their consulting requirements. In 1931, ADL narrowly escaped from bankruptcy when its president, Earl Stevenson, earned a $50,000 bonus from Lever Brothers for testifying in a patent infringement suit. This was $5,000 more than ADL's net profit for the year.

During the next fifty years, there were cycles when the business for some of ADL's practice areas was down. Conservative managers, like Treasurer Paul Littlefield and CEO John Magee, kept the Company on a straight financial track. During their tenure, no consideration was given to new debts that did not have a clear basis for paying them off.

In the early sixties, ADL was suffering from a condition that is typical of professional service companies—collecting on receivables was not keeping pace with payroll costs. This required significant borrowing at a time when interest rates were high. ADL went public to improve its cash position, and the employees could buy up to 120 shares each. The stock went up briefly but then came down again.

In 1988, after surviving a take-over attempt, the Company borrowed $30 million to buy back its stock from the public. It was a good deal for ADL because, by now, the stock was worth only about half of its offering price. Furthermore, the loan was secured through the ESOP employee investment plan. Since the Government gave some tax relief to the participating banks, ADL was able to get a very low interest rate. The existing employee investment plan which had been funded with 5% of the payroll, was discontinued. The money saved by this move was used to pay off the loan.

Despite the careful financial planning, this period was not without difficulties, as declining business in the US caused capital short-ages. In 1988, the write-offs and labor overruns in ADL sections and offices around the world amounted to a staggering $10 million. To cope with the resulting cash flow problems, it was necessary to bring back to America all the profits generated from the increasingly more successful European operations. This constrained the European operations and prevented ADL Europe from becoming a leader in management consulting. Once counted as number two or three among the top consultants in Germany, ADL fell to the sixth position.

In the mid-nineties, ADL needed funds to buy back from the MDT stock to reward senior staff members and European managers who had become increasingly unhappy with the management in Cambridge. For this purpose, the Company sold some existing debt to Aetna and obtained a loan of $35 million.

Some believe that the tipping point that led ADL to its rapid downslide was a $40 million line of credit that the Company obtained in 1998 from lenders led by Citibank. Amended in April 2000, the loan agreement increased ADL's borrowing costs to 12.5%. As business continued to deteriorate and the Company's financial position took a dramatic downturn, the loan covenants with Citibank were violated, and the loan was called. Some believe that, at this point, the Company could have threatened bankruptcy and hoped that Citibank would find it more advantageous to renew the loan. However, ADL turned to less conservative financing instead.

Selling the Acorn Park headquarters in Cambridge was another poorly executed move. A developer offered $20 million for the property and offered to lease new space that he was developing in Watertown. Under pressure for cash, ADL went along with the sale at such a bargain price that the Board was accused of gross negligence and some even questioned whether insiders had made a profit on it.

Many staff members were not happy with the proposed relocation and the business conditions did not justify the high moving cost. ADL was forced to abandon the idea of moving and to lease back its former space from the new owners at high cost. For a time, ADL was able to sublease some of the Watertown space, but the technology downturn left it with a lot of vacant space and little rental income. The property became a significant cash drain.

In mid-1999, with the financial picture continuing bleak and the European staff complaining about mismanagement, the Board looked for a new CEO who would be a strong leader, cut costs, and restructure the Company. They thought they found such a person in Lorenzo Lamadrid, a 50-year-old who had been a classmate of George W. Bush at Harvard Business School and had previously worked for Western Resources International, General Electric and the Boston Consulting Group.

While he was offered a salary of $1 million a year, Lamadrid's real incentive was a deferred compensation plan that depended on the future value of the ADL stock. This meant that he was primarily interested in increasing the value of the firm, and this was probably the reason why he paid more attention to packaging ADL's activities for the stock market than to improving its consulting operations.

Lamadrid's plan for ADL included two thrusts. The first and most immediate one was to reduce costs and improve the Company's financial condition. He brought in another former General Electric

Company executive as treasurer and instigated the biggest personnel layoff in ADL's history. More than 300 people lost their jobs, and the Environmental Consulting practice that had prospered in the preceding years was cut in half.

Lamadrid's second thrust was to make ADL more commercially focused by trying to get revenue from technologies developed in its research labs. In a talk to the MDT group, he said ADL had developed many technologies that had been paid for as professional services but the real money had been left on the table. He gave the American Airlines SABRE reservations system as an example. Here, ADL had generated consulting fees but had gained nothing from the system that was now worth billions. He said he would seek to earn not only professional service fees, but also seek equity participation in such deals. The fact he did not consider was that ADL had been lucky enough to wrestle the SABRE job from stiff competition, and trying to negotiate an equity deal would have killed the opportunity.

To increase the value of ADL stock, Lamadrid wanted to package pieces of ADL and go public with them, hoping to make large profits in the market. In 2000 alone, he planned to bring four ADL subsidiaries to the public. First was the fuel cell technology where ADL had some significant patents for the production of hydrogen. Next, with the hi-tech bubble still rising, he focused on spinning out the Company's highly successful Telecommunications, Information Technology, Media, and Electronics practice and selling a minority interest in this new entity to the public via an IPO. The new company was positioned "to help companies in the wireless and broad-band communications technology industries to identify and implement strategies to exploit opportunities in digital networks and mobile commerce."

C-quential, as the spin-off was named, required significant investment before it could be presented as a freestanding entity. ADL claimed that in 1999, c-quential activities accounted for about one-sixth of its total revenue, but some say that most of this was achieved through fancy accounting to make the IPO more attractive. As the IPO date approached, nearly seven hundred ADL staff members in 30 ADL offices worldwide had been assigned to the project. Sometimes, crude walls were set up to separate them from their colleagues. The cost of the project eventually amounted to about $40 million—equal to the Citibank loan that triggered ADL's financial woes.

In the background, another problem was in the making. By August of 1999, Lamadrid became concerned with the heavy dependence of ADL on the European directorate. This group had contributed most of the profits in the first half of the year and continued to deliver increasing growth and market penetration at a time when the rest of ADL struggled and showed no clear sign of recovery. He noted a high level of dissatisfaction among the leaders and senior managers of the European directorate.

A letter had been delivered to the ADL Board from the European senior managers expressing concerns of governance, but focusing for the most part on the failings of the previous management team. Charlie LaMantia had required the European managers to buy ADL stock, but he did not let them participate in the governance of the Company. This issue was closely tied to the European distrust of the MDT, which held the majority ownership of the Company.

A former Harvard Business School professor was engaged to analyze the situation. He found a high degree of dissatisfaction among the leadership group in Europe and pointed out that there were no non-competition agreements with many of the key personnel.[1] Others were saving on taxes by working as contractors. While this situation had been recognized earlier and efforts had been initiated to mitigate it, there was still a serious risk of a massive defection of the European principals either by forming their own company or joining one of the competitors.

As a result of this analysis, ADL's equity structure was revised and the common stock held by MDT was replaced with preferred stock. The ownership share of the Europeans was increased from 10% to about 24%. In addition, a Global Management Consulting practice was set up to leverage ADL's European strengths and to improve communication between the industry practices, functional practices and markets. To manage this practice, a Global Leadership Team was established consisting predominantly of senior managers from Europe Consulting.

In early 2000, with the European crisis resolved, the subsidiary formations under way and the technology bubble still growing, Lamadrid felt pretty confident. He organized a lavish party in Barcelona to bring together the key c-quential staff from all parts of the world. Several hundred scooters were ordered to be given away as party favors.

---
[1] The use of such agreements in Europe is restricted.

Even without lavish parties, separation of the c-quential activities from the parent company was an expensive undertaking. For the $40 million invested ADL had hoped to raise $150 million through the IPO. However, before all the necessary elements were in place, the telecommunications boom had started to cool down. By the fall, ADL had to cut its expected return from the IPO by a third. But even at the lower price, Wall Street investors, who had begun to shun the entire hi-tech consulting sector, viewed c-quential unfavorably.

The Company gets into deep water

With cash flow running short, the Citibank loan agreement was amended and, as of April 2000, the borrowing costs went up. By January 2001, ADL found itself in a situation where it had defaulted in two ways. It failed to meet the measurements of financial health intended to ensure that the Company could meet its obligations, and it missed principal payments. Soon thereafter, ADL withdrew the IPO for c-quential. The Company was now deeply in debt with no real plan to pull out of it.

Lamadrid had another idea. During the previous year, there had been negotiations to bring in an English firm, PA Consultants, as a strategic partner. These efforts had not been successful. Now, as the financial problems kept increasing, Lamadrid proposed to package all of ADL's professional services practices and sell them to PA. The negotiations with PA Consultants broke off in De-  cember, but resumed again in February when the English sent a team to Cambridge to carry out due dilligence. A few days before they were to arrive, a furious ADL Board had a meeting at which they placed Lamadrid on leave.[2]

Pamela McNamara, formerly head of the firm's North American Management Consulting directorate and the leader of its health care practice, was appointed acting CEO. In a published statement, she tried to strike an optimistic note stressing the Company's "exceptional upside potential" and noted that the firm's "core consulting operations improved significantly over the prior year." Unfortunately, the improvement was not adequate to resolve the immediate financial problems.

In June 2001, Citibank refused to extend its loan. In a frantic and, as it turned out, a fatal step, ADL turned to Cerberus Capital Management—an agressive New York hedge fund that specializes in buying up troubled companies. Cerberus fills a niche in the financial world but it had never dealt with a company that did not have a hard asset base. For this reason, its entry into this situation could be viewed as irresponsible. Nevertheless, ADL borrowed $44 million from Cerberus and used part of the proceeds to repay Citibank. However, the Cerberus loan was much more expensive than the previous loan. ADL had to pay a $1 million closing fee and a $25,000 quarterly administration fee. The interest rate was raised to12%. ADL also had to pay 0.5% interest on a credit line of $85 million which it did not use. The only logic for entering into such an arrangement was the hope of finding a white knight that would lead ADL out of its dilemma.

> The value of ADL stock was reviewed twice each year by an impartial firm. Their value plunged 97% to 15 cents a share from January to June 2001. Subsequently, questions have been raised as to the validity of the valuations and whether the shares at that time had any value at all.

---

[2] Lamadrid was terminated a few months later. ADL satisfied his claim for a severance payment in the amount of $2.3 million over five years. Only a fraction of this had been paid by the time of the bankruptcy.

For about two years, ADL had unsuccessfully searched for a possible merger partner with Lehman Brothers as its investment banker. None of the proposals had worked out. The prospective partners seemed to be confused by the complexity of ADL's far-flung operations and lack of a clear business strategy. For a while, the UK consulting group, PA Consultants, looked like a good prospect, but it fell through because ADL did not want to lose its identity in the merger process. Negotiations took place off and on, and when ADL continued to look for other candidates, PA sued ADL for disregarding an exclusivity agreement between the two companies.

In August of 2001, ADL replaced Lehman with Houlihan Lokey. Instead of trying to sell the company to other large consulting firms, ADL told them to sell the Company to an investment group that ADL had identified and that was led by Whitney & Co. and Safeguard International Fund. ADL expected that the deal would be closed by the end of the year. While this was going on, business continued to slow down and ADL missed a principal payment to Cerberus due in November. However, the expectation of an imminent sale of the Company had put this problem on the back burner.

At that time, the three more technologically oriented lines of ADL business had reached or exceeded their targets for contribution margin. This, however, was not enough to put the Company's finances on track, considering the ongoing restructuring costs and the professional fees associated with them. The one business area that did not meet its target was Global Management Consulting. As a stopgap measure, management published guidelines to stop or severely cut back on all non-client travel, recruiting and training, marketing, and capital expenditures. Strict controls were imposed on the use of subcontractors and external clients on non-client work, other contracted services, leased equipment, and office space. The management consulting practice was restructured to focus on the higher performing areas of business. This included trimming excess capacity, closing or downsizing offices in some markets, and completing the integration of c-quential.

In August 2001, the ADL Board appointed Pamela McNamara as CEO, and directed management to work out the details for exclusive negotiations with Mercer Consulting as a strategic partner. One fact that made any negotiations difficult was that the completion of the year 2000 audit report had been delayed. One of the reasons for the delay was said to be the fact that management wanted the auditors to drop a statement that the Company's operations were in jeopardy. Obviously, inclusion of such a statement in the audit report would not have been seen as a positive statement, especially at a time when ADL was trying to find a strategic partner or sell out. Eventually, the negotiations with Mercer were terminated.[3]

As ADL was groping for new business, it sometimes ventured into subject areas that would have been rejected in better days. The Company came into a flood of criticism in 2001 when it conducted a study for the Philip Morris tobacco company. In the study, that was done in Czechoslovakia, ADL consultants figured out how much money early deaths saved on health care expenses, housing for the elderly, social security and pension.

The ADL report concluded that the early deaths of smokers had positive effects that more than counteracted the medical costs of smoking induced diseases. The report also noted that replacing those who die early leads to savings in social benefits paid to the unemployed and in costs of re-training. The consultants calculated that in 1999, despite the health care costs for dying smokers, the Czech government had a net gain in the amount of $147.1 million, or $1,227 per dead smoker.

Philip Morris proudly informed the Czech government that this represented a pretty good return. The consultants added that the savings to the state for the year were only one part of the positive effect, as one should extend the savings estimate to future years during which the deceased persons would have lived.

In December of 2001, ADL missed another payment to Cerberus making the financing even more expensive. According to the terms of

---

[3] Mercer was interested in ADL's management consulting and not technology business. In retrospect, it would have been wise to sell off the management consultants and use any proceeds to build up the traditional ADL technology business.

the agreement, the interest rate was increased by one percent each month with ADL having to pay monthly extension fees. These started at $500,000 and grew by $500,000 each month, escalating to $3.5 million in June. Furthermore, if ADL did not make up the missed payments by February 15, 2002, Cerberus would take over the Company.

These developments coincided with the collapse of a deal to sell majority interest in the Company to a group of investors led by Whitney & Co. and Safeguard International Fund LP. Faced with an impossible situation, the ADL Board removed CEO Pamela McNamara and hired turnaround specialist Richard Sebastio[4] as the chief restructuring officer. A week after his arrival, the Company filed for bankruptcy.

Additional comments

Following the bankruptcy sale of substantially all of ADL's operating assets, the Company's name was changed to Dehon,[5] Inc. Over the next few years, it figured as the plaintiff in lawsuits reflecting on the actions taken before the bankruptcy.

A key premise in these lawsuits was that ADL had been actually insolvent since mid-1999 or had been rendered insolvent by the actions taken, by engaging into transactions for which the Company's assets were unreasonably small, or by incuring debts beyond its ability to pay as they became due. During such a difficult time, the Board owed its stockholders, its creditors and the entirety of the ADL enterprise the fiduciary duties of good faith, due care and loyalty. The lawsuits brought by Dehon, Inc. claimed that the Board's fiduciary duties were breached.[6]

---

[4] Sebastio came from a crisis management and turnaround firm based in Newport RI and had worked with Nobody Beats the Whiz, a New Jersey electronics retailer, and This End Up, a furniture store in Richmond VA.

[5] The name of the temporarily surviving entity had to be different from "Arthur D. Little" that was acquired by Altran. Dehon was Dr. Little's middle name.

[6] Ironically, the insurance company that was supposed to cover the Board of Directors had sold the incorrect type of policy. It was also served with a lawsuit.

Despite the poor financial condition, the ADL Board had approved a $1.5 million dividend payment to the MDT, as well as more than $1 million in stock repurchase payments to four senior executives at a time when the value of such stock should have been zero.[7] The ongoing lawsuits claimed that the recipients of such distributions had been unjustly enriched because they received payment on equity interests having no value while creditors remained unpaid and subsequently terminated employees did not receive any distribution on their equity interests.

The bankruptcy law also sets limitations on the financial transactions that might take place on or within one year before the petition date, known as the insider preference period. Some obligations to directors were settled during this time at their full value which would have been drastically reduced after the bankruptcy. The lawsuits called for repayment of such amounts.

---

[7] The total amount of such stock re-purchases between September 1999 and September 2001 amounted to nearly $7 million.

CHAPTER 13

The Bankruptcy

"This was terrible management. It was a management-consulting firm that did not consult themselves. A complete implosion. Talk about a tragedy."[1]

On February 5, 2002, ADL announced that it had signed a definitive agreement, subject to bankruptcy court approval, to sell all of the assets of the Company and its subsidiaries to an affiliate of Cerberus Capital Management LP. Pamela McNamara, who had been removed as CEO just a few days earlier but remained a director, told reporters that the deal was "the cornerstone of a new future for Arthur D. Little." At the same time, however, she conceded that the bankruptcy would wipe out shareholder values, including her own shares that represented ninety percent of her net worth.

Cerberus Chief Executive Stephen Feinberg figured that he had the deal all tied up. He issued a statement in which he said that he looked forward to playing an active role in guiding the firm to further growth and profitability and to achieving its full potential in the marketplace. These were his famous last words.

Much against Feinberg's wishes, groups of ADL managers — primarily in Europe, saw that the company was going to be taken for peanuts and feverishly sought financing to outbid him. When the bankruptcy sale took place two months later, Andrew Torgove, senior vice president of ADL's investment bankers, Houlihan Lokey,

---

[1] Andrew Torgove, senior vice president of Houlihan Lokey Howard & Zukin, as quoted in "A Little Goes a Long Way", *The M&A Journal*, Vol.3 No.7

was quoted as saying it was the "most hellacious auction" he had ever seen.

The "hellaciousness" of the auction had much to do with the nature of the procedures that had to be followed. The main purpose of the bankruptcy law is to protect the creditors, and it is a very specialized field that does not always follow the same rules as other legal deliberations. Complex bankruptcies often require large teams of specialized lawyers and they take time. In ADL's case, there was no time as staff members were sending out resumes looking for new jobs.

Aside from the lawyers, other important players in bankruptcies often include investment bankers, any debtors-in-possession, and unsecured creditors. In the ADL case, there were all of these. Baker & McKenzie who had acted as counsel for ADL since 1959, had 187 lawyers on assignment. Goodwin Procter who was appointed as the bankruptcy lawyer, clocked more than 9000 hours of legal work. Houlihan Lokey, the ADL investment banker, dealt with hundreds of potential buyers, executed nondisclosure agreements, and carried on the due diligence process. Cerberus Capital Management, the debtor-in-possession, was looking after his own interests, while the Creditor's Committee represented various unsecured creditors, the largest of which was ADL's ESOP with a claim of $4.4 million.

Because of the complexity of the case and its urgency, high demands were also placed on infrastructure and supporting services. Secure facilities had to be set up where potential buyers could inspect more than 1500 files. Since each bidder group would require its own telephones, printers and fax machines, appropriate space had to be located in the offices of the bankruptcy lawyers, and hundreds of feet of cable had to be strung. Secretarial staff needed to be available around the clock, and the catering people had to provide meals, as well as snacks well into the night.

Once all the facilities were geared up and the various talents were in place, the bankruptcy team was faced with the determination of what it was that ADL had on the block. An identification of ADL's lines of business was important so that the bidders could narrow their bids to businesses that were relevant to them rather than having to bid for the whole enterprise and then sell off the unwanted units.

In previous chapters, we have seen how the organization was continually changed, new subsidiaries formed, and assets re-assigned.[2] ADL had grown into a worldwide conglomerate that had offices in 29 countries. It included several consulting businesses that focused on overlapping industries, a research and development division, a host of independent investments including two international venture capital funds,[3] about 2,000 patents, as well as numerous copyrights and other intellectual property. Contractual lines within the Company were loose, with client contracts sometimes held by one organizational unit while the staff of another unit performed the work. This complexity made the asset identification task exceedingly difficult.

Another factor that contributed to the incredible complexity of the case was the fact that ADL's assets were spread over 44 jurisdictions around the world and across all time zones. For example, anyone who has ever gone through the process of notarizing and legalizing a document intended for a country that is not a party to the Hague Convention, will appreciate the difficulty of assigning ADL's trademark and domain names to their new owners. The fact that ADL's activities stretched across many time zones complicated the negotiations even more.

The Cerberus factor

The involvement of Cerberus at the start of the bankruptcy did not make things any simpler.[4] The idea at the time was that to prevent people from leaving the Company, a message should be sent to the staff that the Company was going to survive one way or another. This would be accomplished by Cerberus taking a position that was referred to as the stalking-horse.

While in Greek mythology Cerberus was the three-headed dog guarding the gates of the underworld, the company that carried its name

---

[2] It has been reported that when the various entities were listed during the bankruptcy process, ADL's treasurer was surprised to find one division that he did not even know existed.

[3] These included a $3 million investment in a Korean venture fund.

[4] Cerberus Capital Management of New York was the principal entity in ADL financing, but its various partner firms became involved at some point during the bankruptcy proceedings. For the sake of simplicity in this chapter, all the entities are referred to as Cerberus.

was even more aggressive. With the bankruptcy, Cerberus was torn between the need to have its loan repaid and its desire to purchase the Company. The negotiations with Cerberus occurred over a period of weeks during which Cerberus took the roles of both a lender and a buyer. As a buyer of ADL, Cerberus drove a hard bargain and used its substantial leverage against ADL to avoid taking on any liabilities or obligations. On the other hand, Cerberus was aware that the purchase agreement it was negotiating would serve as the baseline for future bids for ADL in the bankruptcy sale and, if they aimed too low, competitors could easily outbid them.

ADL and its consultants had estimated the fair value of the Company's assets at about $100 million. After difficult negotiations, the Cerberus partners agreed to pay $71 million, thus setting a price that the auction had to beat. Since ADL was rapidly running out of operating funds, Cerberus also agreed to provide financing until completion of the sale.

While this move permitted management to tell the employees that the Company would not be dissolved, the message did not sit well with the Creditors' Committee. Not having been part of the negotiations, they got the idea that management was selling out to the secured lenders and they would end up with empty pockets.

As a consequence, when ADL asked the bankruptcy judge to approve the deal with Cerberus and require that its bid be held up at the auction as the one to be beaten, the Creditors' Committee objected and asked the judge not to approve the proposed action. This time, the judge disagreed with the committee, and the stalking-horse bid became the reserve price for the auction. In retrospect, one can say that if this had not happened, the sale would not have gone off as well as it did.

Despite such occasional disagreements, the Creditors' Committee played a major role in the success of the auction. In the early stages of the bankruptcy, it made an important decision to withhold the final acceptance of the debtor's proposed reorganization strategy. In this manner, the committee kept the bidders on edge by threatening that they would call for reorganization if the bids were not high enough. Although the committee ultimately decided to support the auction results, its actions resulted in a higher recovery for creditors.

The auction process[5]

Because ADL was a consulting firm whose principal assets were its staff members, speed was critical to the completion of the sale. By the beginning of April 2002, it was clear that the Company would not be able to meet its payroll. Because of these time pressures, the Bankruptcy Court judge ordered that all offers must be submitted by April 2, 2002 and any auction would begin the following day.

ADL's Board of Directors brought in Richard A. Sebastio and his team from RAS Management to drive the sale process and restructuring effort. ADL's own management team was responsible for gathering and organizing the information about the Company's legal structure, so as to provide bidders with complete and accurate information.

The bankruptcy sale took place in the Boston offices of Goodwin Procter. When the purchase offers started to arrive on Monday,

---

[5] Many of the details in this section come from articles in the September 2002 *Newsletter of the Bankruptcy Law Section of the Boston Bar Association*, as well as *The M&A Journal*, Vol. 3 No.7 (see Bibliography).

April 1, they were not encouraging. Only nine bids were received, ranging from offers for specific intellectual property to multiple business units. Since several lines of business had only one initial bidder, it appeared that they would go at unreasonably low prices. Most importantly, nobody tried to beat the $71 million purchase price by Cerberus, and the results did not look good for the unsecured creditors.

Not to be discouraged by the poor showing, the bankruptcy lawyers and ADL managers held day-and-night meetings with each bidder in an attempt to increase their initial bids and generate competitive bidding. The Creditors' Committee supported this effort by threatening to remove certain assets from the sale if adequate bids were not received. They said they would oppose the sale and reorganize the Company if a transaction would not provide an immediate and meaningful dividend to unsecured creditors.

While the negotiations were taking place, the bankruptcy attorneys and the investment bankers reviewed each of the bids to determine whether they qualified under the bidding procedures. Eight bids, including the Cerberus bid, were deemed qualified and the auction opened with a total aggregated bid price of $87,255,000.

While the auction lasted 48 hours, the bidding process itself took only about two hours. This was because the lawyers had to clarify many procedural points and the proposed purchases, as well as resolve potential conflicts over the bidding tactics of some of the bidders.

An unusual incident happened in the evening before the final plan was to be presented to the bankruptcy judge. A Cerberus executive received a call on his cell phone from a senior employee of the Chemical Energy Vertical unit telling him that he and some of his partners would quit if Cerberus won the bidding. They would continue to work only if the successful bidder was Charles River Associates. Since the employees were a key component of the value of the business, this defection would have seriously undermined the value of the business unit. ADL was advised of the call and mounted a feverish round-the-world telephone campaign to all the involved partners of the unit. Faced with criminal penalties for obstructing the bankruptcy, the partners retracted their position. Ironically, it was Charles River Associates that got the unit anyway.

At the conclusion of the auction, the winners lined up as follows:

Altran Technologies and a consortium of entities formed by some of the foreign branch managers bought (a) Global Management and Consulting that was ADL's worldwide management consulting practice, (b) the Eurasian portion of the Global Environment & Risk practice that provided worldwide environmental and risk management consulting services, (c) rights to the Arthur. D. Little name, and (d) Cambridge Consultants, a technology consulting company located in Cambridge, U.K. that focused on product and process design and development. The winning bid was $56 million.

ICF Consulting Group bought the Public Sector Program Management business that concentrated on Government contracts. It also bought the Global Environment & Risk Americas business. Its bid was $10.5 million.

Navigant Consulting bought the Advanced Energy Systems business that worked on strategic decision-making in the electric power and related industries. Its bid was $6,059,972.

TIAX LLC bought the Technology and Innovation practice that included laboratories in Cambridge, Massachusetts and Cupertino, California. Its bid was $16,527,197.

Charles River Associates bought the Chemical Energy Vertical business that emphasized energy consulting for the petrochemical industries. Its bid was $6,966,513.

The auction yielded $96 million for the estate, with $15–20 million in assets still left to be sold. The investment bankers figured that the entire transaction, excluding any assumed liabilities, was worth between $140 and $150 million, as com-pared to the Cerberus offer of $71 million.

The closing

Following the auction, purchase agreements with the five winning bidders had to be executed before the bankruptcy judge would enter an order approving the sales. This process, which took nearly four weeks, was just as complicated as the auction itself.

One of the first issues was who was going to get the exclusive rights to the Arthur D. Little name. This was not of great importance to buyers who were going to integrate the ADL business units with their own, but it was important to others. For example, what was the value of the Arthur D. Little Management Education Institute if it became a generic business school? While Altran acquired the rights in "ADL" and "Arthur D. Little", it was not an easy process. Each trademark and domain name would have to be individually assigned in dozens of jurisdictions, requiring notarization and legalization. It was even more difficult to transfer domain names because the assignee had to have the technology to actually run the site. In some countries, a domain name could be assigned only if the assignee had a local presence.

Another challenge came up in assigning the ownership of the various consulting contracts. The new owners could not assume government contracts without approval, and it was not at all sure that such approval would be granted. Many of the private sector contracts were recorded at a branch or subsidiary being acquired by one buyer but were being performed by a business unit to be acquired by another. It was difficult to sort out such contracts between the buyers, as some of them were unwilling to agree to subcontract portions of the contracts they had purchased. The bank-ruptcy judge eventually resolved the issue by ruling that buyers would subcontract to those who had traditionally done the work.

Disagreements also existed as to the exact nature of the assets that were being transferred. Such matters could not be resolved in the short time span leading to the execution of the purchase agree-ments. The Company and the prospective buyers continued nego-tiations right up to the day of the closings.

The final transaction was the agreement with Altran that called for the transfer of assets and stock in 26 foreign jurisdictions. From the buyer's viewpoint, the transaction was a management buyout. Approximately 200 local ADL managers in various jurisdictions had formed new corporate entities funded by Altran. These foreign buyers were to purchase either the stock of the local subsidiary or the assets of the branch of the relevant debtor. The intellectual

141

property and inter-company debts were to be transferred to Altran directly. As between Altran and the new entities, Altran had the right to take them over after one year.

After all the issues seemed to be resolved, another complication emerged shortly before the closing. A quick-thinking Belgian employee attached all the assets of the Belgian branch of one of the debtors. Since it was important to sell the assets free and clear of encumbrances, the most expedient solution was to negotiate a quick settlement with the employee.

The negotiations with Altran took place in Paris, and it was not until the day before the closing, when somebody pointed out that executing the documents in France would incur significant asset transfer taxes. After a frenzied discussion, it was agreed to perform the actual signing of the documents outside France. In the dark of the night, the closing documents were rushed to Frankfurt. It took an exhausting 15 hours for the representatives of the various parties to sign all the documents.

The auction yielded $96 million for the estate, with $15–20 million in assets still left to be sold. The investment bankers figured that the entire transaction, excluding any assumed liabilities, was worth between $140 and $150 million, as compared to the Cerberus offer of $71 million.

At the end, the lawyers' fees came to a sizeable sum. According to court papers, Goodwin Proctor alone received nearly $6 million and was asking for $1.6 million more. Still, the contracts resulting from the bankruptcy procedures left many items open to interpretation and led to numerous lawsuits.

CHAPTER 14

The Sunday Auction

On the last Sunday in December 2002, about a hundred people filed into the ballroom of the Colonial Hotel in Lynnfield, Massachusetts. Nearly half of them were former ADLers and their spouses who had come to see, if not to bid on, some of the last ADL assets to go on the auction block.

The auction of "memorabilia and ephemera" was conducted by Kaminski Auctioneers & Appraisers. The 461 lots offered for bids included the Board Room portraits of Arthur D. Little, Gen. James Gavin, CEOs Raymond Stevens, John Magee, and Charles LaMantia. Items of unique interest included the silk purse created from a sow's ear, documentation of the lead baloon race, and early correspondence of Arthur D. Little.

During the year preceding the auction, a group of ADLers, including John Magee, had painstakingly catalogued 130 boxes of memorabilia left behind after the sale of the Company. Attempts had been made to find a home for the items without going to a public auction, but the bankruptcy judge wanted to take the path that would bring the most return to the creditors.

Some of the items on the list were curious. For example, there was a 1976 letter designating the ADL building at Acorn Park as a National Historic Landmark. A 1947 history of ADL was marked "Not for Publication." What surprised the ADLers most was a box of World War I wooden ration tokens and 52 lots of postage stamps. Had secretaries saved the stamps from incoming mail or were they left behind by some executive? As it turned out, the auctioneers had thrown these items in to make the proceedings more interesting to the general public.

Also, prior to the auction, ADLers contacted families related to Arthur D. Little and former ADL executives with the intention that they or their representatives would bid on the portraits and other personal materials. One ADLer recalled going to school with one of General Gavin's daughters. Another had run into the grand nephew of Dr. Little on a New Hampshire golf course. Both connections worked, and both families were represented at the auction. Former Senior Vice President Reid Weedon was set up with $20,000 to represent MIT in acquiring materials for its archives.

When the auction started, attention was drawn to bidder #323. Neither he nor his female companion looked familar, so it was assumed he had nothing to do with the Company. However, it was soon obvious that he was after some of the same items as Reid Weedon, and he outbid him every time. Altran had placed a $5000 bid for the portrait of Arthur D. Little. Actually, this was not the original portrait painted by Margaret Brown that was given to MIT soon after it was completed but a copy com-missioned by ADL after the death af Dr. Little. Also, it was slightly torn in two places. The mysterious bidder got it for $5100.

The silk purse, which at one time had been insured for $40,000, was nearly falling apart.[1] The one pictured in the catalogue was actually the other copy located at the Smithsonian. Nevertheless, the mysterious bidder paid $3400 for it. At that point, somebody recognized that the bidder was Dr. Kenan Sahin who had purchased ADL's Technology & Innovation practice, now operating as TIAX.

Bidding on the board room portraits was done with some reluctance. Others encouraged John Magee to bid on his own portrait,

---

[1] The lights in the ADL Board room where it had been displayed affected the material. The purse was re-plasticized in the seventies and had been stitched back to its original condition. By now, however, it was in need of another restoration.

but he displayed his usual modesty and showed only a mild interest. He did enter a bid, however, and got the portrait for $125, which was less than paid for an ordinary World War I poster that was auctioned off immediately afterwards. The attendees applauded Magee for the purchase.

Charles LaMantia did not attend the auction, but it appeared that a colleague was bidding on his behalf. His portrait went for $400 which was more than some had expected. There was nobody to represent Earl Stevenson, whose family could not be reached, and Ray Stevens who apparently had no children. Their portraits were purchased by dealers for the value of the frames and brought $25 each. At the end, Reid Weedon purchased most of the remaining box lots for MIT at $25 per lot.

Even after the auction, some 11,000 boxes of materials as well as machinery remained in warehouses where they may be held for seven years. One item that was missing was an 8 foot wrought iron acorn that had graced the entrance to the Memorial Park building. It was last seen in the ADL vault after MIT took over the building in 2002, but has since disappeared.

CHAPTER 15

Epilogue

When Arthur D. Little Inc. was broken up and sold in pieces, its legacy was separated in two very different directions. The Company name along with its management and consulting practice went to a group of former ADL managers in Europe where the company is still operating pretty much as before. The Technology & Innovation business that was a much smaller part but represented the roots of the company, went to a relatively obscure 61-year-old scientist named Dr. Kenan Sahin.

Dr. Sahin had been a professor at the MIT Sloan School before starting up his own software firm, Kenan Systems. He sold the company to Lucent Technologies in 1999 for $1.48 billion in stock. From the perspective of his MIT experience, Sahin had always seen two "shrines"—Bell Laboratories and ADL. When he read about ADL's financial problems, he offered to help, but was not welcome, as the bankruptcy discussion was already taking place. He then contacted the firm that was arranging for the sale of ADL and soon realized that what was on the table was much bigger than what he had anticipated. He expressed an interest in buying the ADL Management Education Institute, but found that it was already spoken for.

Sahin then engaged the Boston law firm Hale & Dorr to help him in the acquisition of at least some parts of ADL. In particular, he was interested in the Technology & Innovation practice which he considered "the heart of Arthur D. Little." At that time, a group of senior ADL executives that included John Collins, the managing director of the practice, was trying to find the funding for a management buyout of the unit. Hale & Dorr wanted to assign a score of lawyers and perform due diligence. Sahin turned their proposal down as he already knew that he would be getting into a high risk situation. He wanted to pay for just one lawyer.

After meeting with the ADL management team and finding them all outstanding and dedicated professionals, he formed a limited liability company that he wanted to call TIAC—technology and innovation applications company. Since this name was already taken, he settled for TIAX, a name that takes the "applications to the power of x." This new company successfuly bid for all the physical and intellectual assets of ADL's Technology & Innovation practice, including about 300 employees.

Sahin believes that without TIAX the auction of the company would not have succeeded and Cerberus would have exercised its rights to get it as a secured creditor. He purchased the unit at midnight on Thursday, April 4, 2002. He took Friday off but showed up for work at his new company on the following Monday. The receptionist did not know what to do and issued him a visitor's pass. The staff members were similarly confused: what was this guy up to, who would be coming with him?

The following day he and John Collins met with the entire staff in the cafeteria and declared that this was now a small company with a big punch. There would be no management layers to which to pass any blame. The staff liked what they heard and, over the next few months, only about six percent decided to leave. Some were terminated because they were consultants rather than scientists or engineers. Also, the units dealing with telecommunications and information technology were eliminated, since Dr. Sahin considered those areas as overcrowded and requiring a critical mass to be successful.

The next job for the new company was to convince the clients of the former ADL that there would be no change in the professional and work relationships. The existing client contracts had been taken over by TIAX at the time of the sale, but the government contracts could not be sold. They could only be assigned by the government.

While the private sector clients readily accepted the change, it was a problem for the government. Since TIAX was not officially a successor to ADL, it was seen as an unknown entity that had suddenly shown up without any government experience. To make things worse, nobody had thought of informing the government of the events at ADL. Eventually, after a federal audit, the matter was resolved and the former ADL contracts were assigned to TIAX.

Dr. Sahin was interested in preserving some of the legacy of ADL and it was therefore fitting that, at the Sunday auction, he bought the silk purse made from sows' ears. After acquiring the unique item, he found that the plastisizer that held the strands together had deteriorated and, like ADL itself, the purse was falling apart. While he assigned a TIAX staff member to the task of restoring the purse, it was too late to save the Company that had created it.

Bibliography

Acorn Park Network, The, Newsletter of the ADL Alumni Association, 1990-1995.

Adams, James, *Bull's Eye: The Assasination and Life of Supergun Inventor Gerald Bull*, New York: Times Books, 1992.

"ADL Agrees to Be Sold to Lender, Seeks Chapter 11", *The Boston Globe*, February 6, 2002.

"A Little Goes a Long Way", *The M&A Journal*, International Institute on Mergers & Acquisitions, Vol.3, Nr. 7, October 2002.

Arthur D. Little, Inc., *Annual Reports*, 1978-1990.

"Arthur D. Little Sold Off In Pieces", *The Boston Globe*, April 6, 2002.

Brand eins Wirtschaftsmagazin, Issue 04, 2002.

Brown, David, "Weapons of Mass Destruction Lurked Near Canadian Border," *The North Star Monthly*, July 2003.

DeValpine, J. E., "ADL—MDT", Speech at ADL Alumni Association meeting, January 1993.

Glosband, J., Doherty, A.R., Holmes, N.S., Manseau, P.M., and Vitello, D.C., "The Arthur D. Little Sale Experience", *Newsletter of the Bankruptcy Law Section*, Boston Bar Association, September 2002.

Goldring, J., Cook, C., Airley, P.,Webb, L., Woods, R., Hodge, L., Allen, D., "From Ears to Purse: the Global Dimension", *Newsletter of the Bankruptcy Law Section*, Boston Bar Association, September 2002.

"In Default on Loans, ADL Goes on Block", *The Boston Globe*, January 29, 2002.

Kahn, E.J. Jr, *The Problem Solvers: The Inside Story of Arthur D. Little, Inc.*, Boston: Little, Brown, 1986.

Krebs, William A. W., "Remarks at Meeting of ADL Participating Plan Members", December 10, 1956.

Memorial Drive Trust, *Annual Reports*, 1994-2000.

Rodenhauser Reports, Consulting Information Services LLC, 2001.

Rosner, D.B., Klotz, R., "Trying to Fill the Silk Purse – the Creditors' Committee Perspective", *Newsletter of the Bankruptcy Law Section*, Boston Bar Association, September 2002.

Rothermel, Terry, "Auction of ADL Memorabilia," *The ADL Alumni News*, Winter 2003.

Index

151